HOLDING ON TO HOPE

Janet Seever

Copyright © 2020 by Janet Seever

Layout design and cover by Cindy Buckshon

All rights reserved

ISBN: 9798616507044
Imprint: Independently published

*Dedicated to my son, Tim, and my daughter, Rachel,
who have both been part of this journey*

CONTENTS

Holding on to Hope 6

This Christmas Has 12 Days 8

A Lesson for a Lifetime 11

Making a Difference 15

Welcome to My Menagerie 18

Fire on the Mountain 21

A Night to Remember 23

A Place to Call Home 27

Trust Your Pilot 32

Cheering for Chuck 34

Comfort from Above 38

Exactly the Right Teacher 42

God's Handprints 46

Comfort in Times of Trouble 48

Learning Lasts a Lifetime 50

Our Gentle Little Friend 56

I Choose to Laugh 58

Dark Threads in the Tapestry of Life 60

Things That Have Been Personally Helpful to Us 63

Consider It a Challenge 65

Experiencing God's Faithfulness 72

Just One More Letter 74

Thanks, Dad, Thanks 77

Displaying Godly Contentment 80

No One Will Ever Know 81

Searching for Questions 84

Scattering Seeds to the Wind 87

This is My House 91

The Lord Hasn't Forgotten Me 94

To See Him More Clearly 97

Who Is My Neighbor? 99

Perseverance 103

The Christmas Angel 104

A Glimmer of Hope (Fiction) 109

A Journey Through Time 115

A Rainbow for Jenny 120

Next Exit Grapevine 126

Sarah, Please Come Home 132

Our Times Are in Your Hands 137

Holding on to Hope

When my husband Dennis had his debilitating stroke in 2004, three people sent me the verse Romans 15:13 about hope. I held onto that verse. Hope was what we desperately needed.

May the God of hope fill you with all joy and peace as you trust in him, so that you may overflow with hope by the power of the Holy Spirit. (Romans 15:13 NIV)

We've needed hope when Dennis dealt with bipolar mood disorder, undiagnosed for 20 years, a nearly fatal heart problem and when he had his stroke in 2004. I needed hope when I dealt with my eye problems from 2013 when I had my first cataract surgery and for the next five years. My optometrist counted eight things that were causing a problem with my eyes.

Yet, all through this, God has been faithful. The stories in this book are about our trust in the Lord and the hope that kept us hanging on. They are from all over and have been printed in 13 anthologies and gift books as well as magazines and websites.

So when did I start writing? In 2002, a Christian writer friend of mine told me about a Christian website, worthfinding.com that was looking for stories. As I shared my writing, I always put a copy in a folder marked "Archives." All along I planned to do something with my writing some day and realized that if I didn't do it soon, it wouldn't happen.

Dennis and I joined Wycliffe Bible Translators in 1975, so stories come from Mexico (Jungle Camp training), Papua New Guinea (1977-1980), the Philippines (six months in 1985), Dallas, Texas (at various times), and Darwin, Australia (1986-1990). The most recent ones are from Calgary (1993 to the present time). Dennis had a very large stroke in 2004, lived in a personal care home from 2009 to 2019 and is now in a nursing home. He can no longer walk.

Since not all of the stories are in order, they are labeled with the location and the date. If they were published in a book or magazine, that is given as well. Nearly all of them found a home on the worthfinding.com website.

May you be blessed as you read about our adventures and what the Lord has done in our lives.

The last section of the book is fiction. The ideas for the stories came from real life situations, but the characters are fictional. Amanda Jane in "The Christmas Angel" is based on my relationship with my own grandmother who was a teacher. She told me the war story and was the person who pointed me to Jesus.

In a couple instances, names have been changed. My special thanks to Pat, my skilled editor and proofreader, and to Cindy, my friend who is a talented graphic artist. She encouraged me to put the pieces of this book together and did the layout and design. Thanks also to Doug and Kathy who did proofreading.

May the Lord give you hope in your own life.

This Christmas Has 12 Days

Twinkling lights reflected off the red, green and blue balls on the artificial Christmas tree. Outside a few snowflakes drifted down as the gray Sunday afternoon sky darkened. Night came early in mid-December.

Although it was less than two weeks before Christmas, I found it difficult to be in a festive mood. I went through the motions of putting up a few decorations around the house, but my heart wasn't in it that year.

Our family was going through one of the most difficult years of our lives with major health issues, a serious work-related problem for my husband, and difficulties with our teenage son. Some decisions we needed to make in the months ahead could alter the direction of our lives for years to come.

Yes, Christmas was coming. I knew I should be focusing on the birth of Christ. As a Christian, I should be remembering God's goodness and His blessings, but my focus was often on the overwhelming problems we were experiencing. I often felt numb.

"Mom, I wish we could spend Christmas with Grandpa and Grandma in Minnesota. I miss them, and all of my aunts and uncles and cousins," said Rachel, 15, as she sat on the floor, wrapping a small package for one of her friends. A wave of homesickness swept through me. Because of the distance, we had spent far too many Christmases away from our family.

"I know you'd like to spend Christmas in Minnesota, Rachel. So would I." I looked up from the notes I was writing on my printed Christmas letters. "But Minnesota is 1,200 miles. from Calgary. You remember how hard it was to drive in that snowstorm two years ago. And then the temperature dropped to -30 degrees on the way back."

"I remember. Tim and I almost froze our feet when the heater didn't work well."

We had concluded driving home for Christmas was too

risky. Buying airline tickets for four people was totally out of the question. No one was coming over for Christmas either; I just didn't have the energy to invite anyone. We would be spending Christmas alone.

My thoughts were jolted back to the present when the doorbell rang. It was now dark outside.

"Rachel, will you please get the door?"

By the time she got up off the floor, the doorbell had stopped ringing.

As she opened the door, her voice registered surprise. "Mom, there's a box with presents on the doorstep, but nobody is out here!"

I walked to the door and helped her bring in the box. Who could have left it?

The box contained numerous packages wrapped in bright Christmas paper. Each had a typewritten tag: Open Dec. 15, Open Dec.16. There were a total of 12 — the "12 Days of Christmas." The first day, Dec. 14, was attached to a turkey wrapped in the plastic in which it had come from the store —so we put it in the freezer immediately. Putting it under the tree would have been a mistake!

That day's tag read: Our LOVE is given anonymously,/ So enjoy fun with your family,/ But don't tell anyone please.

Now we were really mystified. Thankful, I put the turkey in the freezer and the rest of the gifts under the tree.

After that, we gathered each day as a family, opened one more tag, read the clever little note inside, and then tried to guess what the package held. It became a game to us. Even our son joined us on occasion. As the days slipped by, we discovered potatoes, sweet potatoes, a package of marshmallows, cranberries, packages of gelatin, pickles, olives, cans of green beans, corn, mints, ginger ale and nuts. Together the packages made a complete Christmas dinner for four people. We opened the last package on December 25.

As we opened each anonymous package, we realized someone was thinking of us, loving us, wishing us a wonderful Christmas. Someone who wished to remain anonymous.

As it turned out, a family from work gave us an invitation for Christmas dinner a few days before Christmas. We ended up celebrating New Year's Day with the goodies which our benefactor had lovingly given us. We were blessed and so thankful to be loved!

In the following years, the Lord helped us unravel the knot of difficulties one by one—many were inter-related. The life-altering decision never had to be made; health issues were diagnosed and treated, a solution was found for the serious work-related problem, and our son outgrew his rebellious teen years. Now, years later, our nightmare year seemed like a distant memory. We've gone through a time of healing as a family.

You're probably wondering if we ever found out who gave us the anonymous Christmas gift. We never did. At first I wanted to know, but later it became unimportant. Now I realize knowing would spoil things. That gift was given out of love with no strings attached, with nothing we could do to deserve it or to pay the person back. It came when we needed a reminder that we were loved. I still have the little tags folded in a page of my journal. What a wonderful memory!

To me, that 12-day gift is like God's Gift at Christmas; with no strings attached, not something we could earn or deserve. Love freely given with no thought of return—that's what Christmas is all about.

Calgary, Alberta,1996
This story appeared in the gift book, Opening the Gifts of Christmas. *A modified version of this story appeared in two* Chicken Soup for the Soul *books in 2017.*

A Lesson for a Lifetime

When I arrived at 6 a.m. in the large hospital kitchen, Rose was already checking name tags on the trays against the patient roster. Stainless steel shelves held rows of breakfast trays that we would soon be serving.

"Hi, I'm Janet." I tried to sound cheerful, although I already knew Rose's reputation for being impossible to work with. "I'm scheduled to work with you this week."

A stocky middle-aged woman with graying hair, Rose stopped what she was doing and peered over reading glasses perched on her nose. I could tell from her sour expression she wasn't pleased to see a student worker.

"What do you want me to do? Start the coffee?" I was feeling less confident by the minute.

Rose sullenly nodded and went back to checking name tags.

I filled the 40-cup pot with cold water and began making the coffee when Rose gruffly snapped, "That's not the way to make coffee." She stepped in and took over.

"I was just doing it the way our supervisor showed us to do it," I said in astonishment.

"The patients like the coffee better the way I do it," she replied curtly.

Nothing I did pleased her after that. All morning her eagle eyes missed nothing and her sharp words stung. She literally trailed me around the kitchen.

Later, after breakfast had been served and the dishes had been washed, I set up my share of trays for the next meal. Then I busied myself cleaning the sink. Certainly Rose couldn't criticize the way I did that.

When I turned around, there stood Rose, rearranging all of the trays I had just set up!

Later at break time, some of the older full-time workers decided to have some fun and started teasing me. "Are you having a good time working with Rose?" Margaret's mischievous blue eyes twinkled as she baited me with her questions.

"That's not even funny," I said, biting my lip to keep back the tears.

Totally exhausted, I trudged the six blocks home from the University of Minnesota Hospital late that June afternoon. As a third year university student working my way through school, I had never before encountered anyone like Rose.

With muscles still tense, I wrestled with my dilemma alone in my room. "Lord, what do you want me to do? I can't take much more of Rose."

I turned the possibilities over in my mind. Should I see if my supervisor would switch me to work with someone else? Scheduling was fairly flexible. On the other hand, I didn't want to be a quitter. I knew my co-workers were watching to see what I would do.

The answer to my prayer caught me completely by surprise—I needed to love Rose.

Love her? No way! Tolerate, maybe, but loving her was impossible. "Lord, I can't love Rose. You'll have to do it through me."

Working with Rose the next morning, I ignored the barbs thrown in my direction and did things her way as much as possible to avoid friction. As I worked, I silently began to surround Rose with a warm blanket of prayers. "Lord, help me love Rose. Lord, bless Rose."

Over the next few days an amazing thing began to happen. As I prayed for this irritating woman, my focus shifted from what she was doing to me, and I started seeing Rose as the hurting person she was. I was the one who changed first, not Rose. As the icy tension began to melt away, Rose criticized less and less.

Throughout the rest of the summer, we had numerous opportunities to work together. Each time she seemed genuinely happy to see me.

"I saw on the schedule they got the two of us working together next week," she would say as we passed in the hospital hallway. "I'm glad about that."

As I worked with this lonely woman, I listened to her—something no one else had done.

I learned that she was burdened by elderly parents who needed her care, her own health problems, and an alcoholic husband she was thinking of leaving. There was no question that her lot in life was difficult, and I began to understand what made her the way she was. I even had an opportunity to tell her that when I had problems, the Lord was my source of strength.

As I listened to her, I discovered her unique way of doing things was because she wanted to do something special for the patients. She explained how her method of setting up trays helped the eye surgery patients on this hospital station to find things more easily on the tray. Cubing the brightly colored gelatin slabs made them look prettier in the bowls and easier for patients to eat. She had her own reasons for everything she did.

In return, she wanted the patients to appreciate her for doing special things for them. This woman—whom I once considered so unlovable— was actually begging for someone to love and appreciate her! I learned so much by observing Rose, far more than anything I learned from a textbook in my years at the university.

The days slipped by quickly as I finished the last several weeks of my summer job. Leaves were starting to turn yellow and red, and there was a cool crispness in the air. I soon would be returning as a full-time student.

One day, while I was working alone in one of the hospital kitchens, Rose entered the room. Instead of her blue uniform, she was wearing street clothes.

I looked at her in surprise. "Aren't you working today?"

"I got me another job and won't be working here no more," she said as she walked over and gave me a quick hug. "I just came to say good-bye." Then she turned abruptly and walked out the door.

Although I never saw Rose again, I still remember her vividly. That summer I learned a lesson I've never forgotten, although nearly 40 summers have come and gone since then. The world is full of people like Rose—irritating, demanding, unlovable—yet hurting inside. I've found that love is the best way to turn an enemy into a friend.

Minneapolis, Minnesota. 1965. This story appeared in Grace Givers, *edited by Dr. David Jeremiah. It appeared on numerous inspirational websites and circulated on Internet.*

Making a Difference

It was very late in the summer of 1970. I was a new teacher with a secondary science degree, desperate for a job. A parochial school in a small town of 1,300 people urgently needed an elementary teacher for geography, math and some science. It wasn't an exact match, but I got the job.

I didn't fit in with the other young lay teachers who, unfortunately, were into the party scene. My closest friend during those school days was a 60-year-old nun, Sister Cecilia, who taught remedial reading. That gives you an idea of what my social life was like.

In days before school started, I decorated my classroom and put potted plants on all of the windowsills. On my first day of teaching, Leslie, a fourth grader who was sitting near the window, pulled plants out of the pots. After I moved him to a different seat, he proceeded to spread his entire bottle of glue over his desk and then dusted chalk from an eraser into it. And that was just the first morning. It was an ominous sign of things to come.

I found that I spent 85 percent of my energy disciplining and 15 percent imparting knowledge. Of course I had some wonderful, serious students who would do well wherever they were in life, but others worked hard to push the limits.

At night I went home exhausted, often near tears. I felt lonely, missing my friends back in the city.

Lord, why am I here? I wondered. *Whatever gave me the idea I wanted to teach?* And then there was Mark. A fourth grader, Mark struggled with school, but in my geography class he always got A's. He studied hard, and always raised his hand in class.

After school Mark would come into my classroom to dust erasers or empty the wastepaper basket, while I was correcting papers and straightening the classroom for the next day. "Why do you come in to visit me?" I asked him one night.

"Because at home there are too many kids, and no one listens to me," was his reply. As I got to know him, I understood his situation. There were 11 children in his family, with Mark near the middle.

At times Mark told me about his philosophy of life, about his family, and his view of God and the world. His chatter was like sunshine on a cloudy day.

One time when he came to see me, he said, "Miss Ausmus, the kids are saying that you and Mr. D. like each other."

"Mark, Mr. D. is a nice man and we both teach some of the same students. We talk to each other about teaching. He is not my boyfriend, and it's not something the children should be talking about anyway."

Thinking a minute, he said, "How do people keep from having babies?"

I was tacking Christmas decorations up on a corkboard and almost fell off my chair.

"Uh. . . Mark, I think the wastebasket needs to be emptied. Could you do that for me please?"

Another time he said, "Will you wait for me so I can marry you when I grow up?"

"Sorry, Mark, but that won't work," I responded sympathetically. "I'm 14 years older than you are now, and I will still be 14 years older when you are grown." Oh, the logic of a nine-year-old boy.

When my birthday arrived, his mother made me a cake. She delivered it after school, and as Mark was carrying it up the school steps, he tripped, dropping the cake. I found him in tears, covered with fluffy white frosting.

I assured him that bringing me a cake was very, very special, whether I was able to eat it or not.

So instead of making another cake, his mother invited me to their home for a meal and I got to know his delightful family.

After my second year of teaching, it was time to move on. I said "good-bye" to Mark and his family. I then invited him and his younger brother to a Bible camp where I was counseling that summer. They came, and I heard from their counselor that both of the boys accepted Jesus as their Savior.

Years passed and in 1992, I went back to the little town to visit. Not much had changed in the 20 years I had been gone. Mark's parents still lived in the same house. Once bursting at the seams and filled with noise and laughter, it was now strangely quiet.

His mother greeted me warmly. I had taught two of her children and knew the others, so she pulled out all of their wedding photos and told me what each was doing.

Mark had graduated from college, married and was working at a good job.

"Janet," she said, "Thanks for all the time you took encouraging Mark. You taught him to believe in himself. You are the reason he went to college."

Those words both surprised and gratified me.

I had made a difference in the life of a young boy. But I wonder—did Mark ever know the difference he made in mine?

1972. Winsted, Minnesota.

Welcome to My Menagerie

Summer had faded into fall in the small Minnesota farming community, bringing hoards of eager and not-so-eager students back to school. Golden fields of wheat had turned into great grasshopper-filled expanses of stubble. Ripened apples hung on the trees, waiting to be picked.

As a young teacher in my second year of teaching, I planned as much hands-on experience as possible for my 5th and 6th grade science classes in this rural setting with its abundance of plants and animals to study.

Not all animals make good pets, of course—some are best left in the wild. However, all can be used to teach respect for all of God's living creatures, great and small. At least that was my theory.

One beautiful fall day, I took my students on a nature hike to a nearby lake where they collected the local flora and fauna. A few brought back frogs, so we looked at characteristics of amphibians.

Someone picked up a fat white, yellow and black caterpillar on a milkweed plant and we marveled at the characteristic pale green Monarch chrysalis in the jar within a few days. One of the boys brought in several garter snakes, which were common in the area, so we placed them in a large glass aquarium with a mesh screen lid.

"These garter snakes are reptiles," I said as I picked up a squirming snake and held it up for my science class to observe. "They have scales and are not slimy like some people think. They are completely harmless." The girls in the class were totally unconvinced and did nothing to hide their dislike for the creatures, to the delight of the boys.

Between class periods, the boys were continually drawn to that aquarium. I was delighted that they were taking such an interest in the snakes, until I later realized just why those snakes were attracting so much attention. As the boys observed the snakes, they made sure they left the lid slightly ajar, allowing the snakes an exit if they found it.

"There's a snake on the floor," screamed one of the girls, jumping up on her chair as others around the classroom gasped and squealed. The boys found it difficult to contain their glee. After that I kept an eye on the snake cage whenever the boys were near it.

One day, however, I wasn't observant enough. I heard a commotion and some screams from across the hallway. Soon there was a knock on my door. Flanked by the principal, Sister Ann pulled herself up to her full height of five feet one inch. Normally a placid person, she now had fire in her eyes. "Either those snakes go . . . or I go!" Her voice was ominous. "One of *your* snakes just crawled under *my* door and terrified my first graders." By noon that day the snakes had won their freedom in a nearby field.

Sometime later one of my students approached me. "We have some gerbils in a large cage at home," said Terri. "My mom says I can bring the cage to school and we can keep them in our classroom."

"Great! That's really a generous offer," I said, looking up from the paper I was correcting. "Tell your mother we would love to have them." Little did I realize just *how* generous the offer was.

Gerbils are cute, friendly and prolific. The huge metal mesh cage, which was on a metal tray, soon became the center of attention. With many eyes peering in and hands reaching into the cage, the five gerbils became a bit nervous, and were no longer prolific.

What messy little creatures they turned out to be! They acted as paper shredders, happily chewing anything that landed in their cage. All of the students were happy to oblige. Many of the homework papers they turned in now were stamped with characteristic teeth marks in a corner, much as we would stamp "received" or "paid" on our paperwork. If a student had a bad test mark, he would accidentally slip the test paper into the cage and presto, it was gone. There was nothing left to take home to his parents.

One day after school, the custodian paid me a dreaded

visit. My heart sank as I saw him walk into the room with a grim look on his face.

Leaning his metal hook hand against his large industrial dust mop, Mr. B. chose his words carefully. "As I sweep up the paper scraps, static electricity makes them cling to my dust mop, and I end up getting them all over the building." He paused, glaring at me. "I will no longer be cleaning your room. You will need to clean it yourself."

So I added sweeping my classroom to the list of tasks I needed to do each afternoon before I could go home.

One day some weeks later, I called Terri up to my desk. "Thanks so much for bringing your gerbils to school so we could see them. We've enjoyed them for a couple months, but now I think it's time for them to go back home."

I'll bet her mother was ecstatic to get the news. I could almost hear her cheering clear across town.

1971 Winsted, Minnesota.

Fire on the Mountain
(Devotional)

Stars were beginning to poke through the darkening southern Mexico sky. Crickets chirped and the high-pitched trill of the cicadas grated painfully on our ears. My husband, Dennis, and I —as well as most of the other missionary trainees—were settling down for the night.

Suddenly the acrid smell of smoke drifted into our adobe thatched-roof house. Where was it coming from?

"Dennis, come quick!" I stared out the doorway. "The whole mountain is on fire!"

Terror gripped my heart. Only a narrow river separated us from the raging blaze less than a mile away. The entire western sky glowed red.

"Let's find someone who knows what's going on!" Dennis raced down the path as I panted to keep up with him. We soon found Frank, one of our training supervisors.

"They burn the mountain every year at this time," he said, his face showing little concern. Then, seeing how frightened we were, he grew serious. "I'm sorry, I thought we had warned everyone. Apparently we missed you."

"Why do they do that? I questioned, my knees still shaking.

"The people in this area practice slash and burn farming," Frank explained. "It's controlled burning."

"Isn't there any other way to farm?" I asked, thinking back to our family farm in Minnesota.

"If you look at the slope of the mountain, you'll notice it's much too steep to plow," Frank continued. "The people plant corn by hand along the slope and harvest the ears by hand as well. Besides, corn stalks don't compost well, and the burning kills the insects which would eat the tender corn seedlings as they emerge."

I was incredulous. "You mean it's necessary?"

"Absolutely. Without the fire, these people wouldn't be able to raise their corn."

Extreme measures—that's what God sometimes uses in our lives. When it seems like He is using His version of "slash and burn," we want to cry out, "Please stop! I can't take any more." The Bible says we are tested and refined: "For you, O God, tested us; you refined us like silver" (Psalm 66:10 NIV). It speaks of disciplining in Hebrews 12:10 NIV: "but God disciplines us for our good, that we may share in his holiness." We are also likened to branches which He prunes: ". . .every branch that does bear fruit, he prunes so that it will be even more fruitful" (John 15:2 b NIV).

Each of these processes is painful, and yet each process makes us holy, refines us and makes us more like Him. God allows each to come into our lives for a purpose.

Are these things necessary? Absolutely. It is only through pruning, refining and disciplining that we fully yield ourselves to Him and lay aside things which hinder us from following Him fully. God's methods may seem like extreme measures, but without them, we wouldn't be fruitful.

Chiapas, Mexico, 1976.

A Night to Remember

"It doesn't seem like Christmas season," I remarked to my husband, Dennis. "I guess if we want a Christmas tree this year, we'll have to use a banana tree."

Instead of the gently falling snow and frosted windows of my Minnesota childhood, tropical downpours pelted our metal roof nightly with a deafening roar. Daytime temperatures soared into the low 90s and the humidity was high.

We had been in Papua New Guinea as missionaries for six months and were adjusting to being away from friends and family for the first time. However, the prospect of holidays without loved ones brought a new wave of homesickness. I couldn't even play my Christmas music tapes because our broken tape recorder was being repaired.

Then an invitation to a children's Christmas program arrived. A month earlier, the international school in town had contacted me when they urgently needed a substitute teacher for a couple of days. As a result, we were invited to the elementary school's Christmas program, and I eagerly accepted. I wanted to see the children I had taught, but more than that, I was eager for something that reflected Christmas, since they would be singing Christmas carols as part of the program.

We normally rode our motorcycle into town during the day, but that night we borrowed a van from friends. Jeannette, who worked with another mission down the road, wanted to ride with us.

The evening was a lovely diversion from the many nights we spent at home. We enjoyed the singing, and visiting with other expatriate families afterward was a high point of our week.

When we began our four miles journey home several hours later, the nightly rain had already started. The swish of the windshield wipers kept a steady pace as the van creaked and rattled along. Dennis carefully dodged the pot holes.

We had gone about four miles when suddenly our

pleasant conversation came to an abrupt halt. As we rounded a bend, lanterns flashed in the darkness, and about 20 shouting and waving Papua New Guinea villagers blocked the road ahead of us.

My muscles tensed as I peered through the rain-spattered windshield. "What do they want?" I asked. These were *not* people we wanted to encounter in the dark. We had been told that during WW 2—more than 30 years earlier—people from this village aided Japanese soldiers, and they were later severely punished by the Australian government ruling Papua New Guinea at that time. For that reason, people from this village hated all white people.

The spokesman for the group told us in broken English that a tree had struck the bridge up ahead. All three of us in the van collectively breathed a sigh of relief—the villagers were only trying to warn us. The human roadblock moved aside and let us pass.

Dennis inched the van slowly forward. How much damage had been done? Could we still get across? Jeannette lived on the other side of the creek and we still had a couple of miles to go beyond that before we reached home.

Our headlights soon revealed the problem. The shallow stream we crossed three hours earlier had become a raging torrent, fed by heavy rain in the mountains. Many of the large trees growing along the creek had shallow root systems and were easily uprooted when the water rose. One of these uprooted trees had rammed the bridge and lay partly over the top of it. The road now ended abruptly with a ten-foot drop where swirling brown water had eroded a yawning hole. A 12-foot gap separated the road from the bridge, rendering it completely useless.

We surveyed the situation with dismay, not wanting to spend the night there—but there was no way to get across.

"I have an idea," said Jeanette. "We could leave the van here and walk across the new bridge." She got her flashlight out from under the seat of the van. "Our mission is only about a quarter of a mile farther."

The new two-lane bridge, 25-feet high, was well above the water level. It ran parallel to the old one and had been under construction for the past seven months. All it needed was the railings.

After Dennis backed up the van and parked it on the muddy shoulder of the road, we all got out. By now the villagers were beginning to construct a barricade with 55 gallon drums to prevent anyone from accidentally driving into the swirling water.

The road leading to the new bridge was not yet graveled, so clods of clay clung to our shoes. The rain had lessened to a gentle mist. Using Jeanette's flashlight to guide us, we slowly started to cross. The angry water roared below us as brush and boulders crashed into the steel bridge pilings.

"Lord, keep us safe," I prayed. "Please help us get home."

The bridge seemed to stretch on endlessly. We could see its outline through the mist as the beam of light bounced off the wet concrete in front of us. Then Jeannette's flashlight started to flicker.

Suddenly we froze in our tracks. Fifteen feet in front of us, there was no more bridge or road—just swirling water 20 feet below! The raging water had changed its course and washed out about 45 feet of land fill and road leading up to the bridge.

With knees shaking and a nearly dead flashlight, we carefully retraced our steps to the parked van.

Then Jeannette had another idea. "A new family just moved into our mission's administrative headquarters near town," she said. "We might be able to spend the night there."

"Good idea," said Dennis. "But first I think we should let the police know the bridge is out." He eased the van out of the mud and headed back to town.

We had gone a couple miles and were nearing town when we discovered two huge trees—the kind with shallow root systems—had fallen across the road we had just traveled 30 minutes earlier.

I gasped. "If we had turned back any sooner we might have been under those trees!"

"The Lord was really watching over us," said Jeannette, echoing the sentiment we all felt.

We spent the night in the mission house as Jeannette had suggested, and the next afternoon the water subsided enough for us to wade across the knee-deep muddy stream.

We learned that bamboo houses had been swept away in several villages, leaving 400 homeless, and one elderly woman had drowned. The water had enough force to move boulders six feet in diameter.

Later I shared the terrifying experience with a friend, but he seemed unimpressed. "A lot of people have narrow escapes every day. Nothing happened to you. It was just an inconvenience not to get home."

Nothing happened? Just an inconvenience? I was indignant. But then I saw what he meant. We had been warned in time and hadn't driven off the bank, we weren't in any real danger of falling off of the bridge, and half a forest could have fallen across the road in the time we were gone. There was no miraculous rescue.

So nothing happened that terrifying night . . . or did it? I am the kind of person who imagines the worst in every situation and could see myself being swept away by raging water or trapped under a fallen tree. What did happen is that I got to know the Lord and His abiding presence in a new way that night. It was as if He tapped me on the shoulder and whispered, "I was right there with you all the time, just as I promised."

Thank you, Lord, for being our Immanuel—God with us—in the difficult times of life.

Papua New Guinea, 1977. Published in Christmas Stories & More, *2017*

A Place to Call Home

I wrapped a clean cloth around my bleeding finger, angry that I had been careless. The machete wound probably wouldn't require stitches, but infection was a real danger in tropical Papua New Guinea. Even mosquito bites and small scratches easily became infected.

"Lord, what am I doing here?" I questioned. "How am I serving You? How does skinning bark off logs have anything to do with mission work?"

New to the field, I was homesick and the knot in my stomach wouldn't go away. At night I dreamed of friends and family back home, only to awaken disappointed that I had been dreaming.

When we had arrived in Papua New Guinea six weeks earlier, my husband, Dennis, and I were assigned to work at Jonita Center, a small regional center providing services for seven translation teams working in the mountainous area nearby. Harry and Natalie, a couple in their 50s, were doing Bible translation at the center. With their other work, they did not have time to meet planes, do buying for teams, maintain the generator, do bookkeeping and care for overnight guests. Those would be our responsibilities. In addition, my husband — trained as an industrial arts teacher— would do some construction, including our house.

When my husband and I arrived at the small airport near Jonita Center in a single-engine Cessna, the heat and humidity overwhelmed us, draining our energy. Doug, a translator we had met previously, was waiting for us in a pickup truck and would be taking us to Jonita Center. We were surprised to see Harry and Natalie in the truck, waiting to board the plane on which we had just arrived.

We knew that Natalie had been ill for some time with a stiff neck and bad headaches which puzzled the local doctor, but her condition shocked us.

"We've decided to go to Ukarumpa to see the doctor there," said Harry as he gently helped his heavily sedated wife out of the truck. (Ukarumpa was the main center with a small clinic.) "We'll probably be gone for three months until Natalie is better. In the meantime, you can live in our house while you're building your own. Just make yourselves at home."

Harry was supposed to supervise our work and tell us how to run the center. Now what? So here we were, skinning bark off logs cut in the jungle to make posts for our house. Before our arrival, an area had been cleared for us in the jungle for our house. Beyond the edge of the clearing, vines wound their way up 60-foot trees and parrots flew, flashing their brilliant red and green colors.

Part of our building material was "bush material" gathered from the jungle, part was off-cut lumber ("seconds") purchased locally, and some lumber had been ordered from a coastal city. The lumber from the coastal city would be brought by boat and then trucked the last 20 miles.

When our shipment of lumber finally arrived, Dennis inspected it. Puzzled, he said, "I *know* I ordered roof rafters and floor joists . . . but this shipment contains *only flooring*." (Months later we discovered that two similar orders were mixed up and both sent to wrong destinations.)

We received updates of Natalie's condition by a two-way radio located in Harry's house in which the two of us were now living. The news wasn't encouraging — she seemed to be getting worse, not better. The mission doctor checked her for encephalitis, cerebral malaria and other possibilities, but without proper diagnostic equipment, he reached a dead end. Harry arranged to take her to Australia for medical help.

Then one day the sad news came. Natalie was diagnosed with an inoperable brain tumor, and the next day she died. We were shocked.

Grieving deeply, Harry made funeral arrangements, and Natalie was buried in the little cemetery in Ukarumpa. He then told us he would be back at Jonita Center in two weeks. We would need other housing — housing which didn't exist.

What would we do? Our money was tied up in building supplies, and house building had reached a standstill without the floor joists and roof rafters. Arranging housing at another mission down the road wasn't practical without transportation. Then we had an idea. With $200 we had left, we put up a 12 by 15 foot workshop to live in temporarily.

In our haste, we had failed to put down a moisture barrier (a sheet of plastic) when pouring the concrete floor— a big mistake. Our floor was always damp; sand in front of the door stuck to our feet and stuck to the damp floor. At night we would brush sand out of our bed with our pillows and would brush our feet off before crawling in, a ritual repeated nightly. The room was constantly damp, and our "Sunday best," would often be freckled with mildew by the next week. Leather belts turned green with mildew after a few weeks. Cockroaches played in the open cupboard Dennis built, and one night a snake slithered up our window screen, looking for an opening between the board and batten walls to squeeze through.

"I hate this place!" I shouted tearfully one night, feeling depressed, and directing my anger toward my shocked husband. "I hate the roaches, the snakes, and the sand. When will I ever have a place I can call 'home'?" For emphasis, I stomped on empty egg cartons I had been saving, and kicked them across the floor. Not only did I *not* feel better, I now felt guilty for my lack of self-control.

Harry resumed his translation. Having completed one New Testament several years earlier, he tackled two related languages with 14-year-old boys as language helpers. He would go over the passage with them, and they changed the words which were different in their own languages.

Natalie had been Harry's typist, and now I took over typing from hand-written copy in the boys' sometimes nearly illegible hand writing. In sweltering 90-degree heat, I used a Remington manual typewriter — it was before the advent of computers and we had only four hours of electricity each day.

While living in Harry's house, I had inadvertently seen

a paper with his request to the branch director for a couple to manage the center. He wanted a 60-word-per-minute typist who would be able to train Papua New Guineans in typing. I had once managed 45 words per minute, and that was in English, not two languages I didn't know. I certainly couldn't train anyone else.

So Harry didn't get his request, and wrapped up in his own grief, he said little about my help. I was certain he was disappointed with me and my ability and I felt so discouraged.

"Lord, why am I here? I'm not at *all* what Harry wanted." I was having difficulty seeing everything which was happening as part of God's plan.

Then one day Jim, our regional director, stopped at our center on his way to the village where he worked. He and his wife, Jaki, had just completed a translation in the Managalasi language.

Just great, I thought. *The last thing I need right now is an evaluation of how we're doing.*

Accepting a cup of tea, Jim sat down at the borrowed table in our crowded little house. "Well, how are things going for you?" he asked in his soft Tennessee drawl. "Are the two of you adjusting to living out here?"

The conversation was strained as I choked back tears.

Sensing our uneasiness, Jim began a story. "You know, when Jaki and I first moved to our village, it was really rough. We were isolated; the villagers didn't understand why we were there. We were often discouraged . . . so discouraged we thought about quitting many times," he said, pausing to reminisce.

"Do you know what made the difference?" he continued. "Chururu, a young village man, was mean and people were afraid of him. But he was the best reader in the village, so we had him check Scripture. After spending so much time reading Scripture, God's Word spoke to him. He accepted the Lord, and his life was completely transformed. He was like a totally different person.

"The Lord used Chururu to show us what we were doing was valuable to Him," said Jim as he finished his tea which had now grown cold. "The Lord wouldn't let us quit."

Then Jim turned to me. "Harry appreciates the typing you are doing. If he didn't have someone to type for him, *he couldn't continue his translation.*" He let the words slowly sink in.

That was a turning point for me.

Nothing in our workshop house changed. The sand and mildew were still there, and the cockroaches still played on the shelves. We ended up living in that workshop for eight months.

I was the one who changed. Suddenly I saw that the Lord was more interested in my availability than my ability. I *was* making a difference . . . a difference for eternity.

1977, Papua New Guinea. Published in Word Alive, *a publication of Wycliffe Bible Translators. The Aneme Wake New Testament, for which I typed the rough draft, was published many years ago and Harry Weimer passed away several years ago. Jim and Jaki Parlier's work with the Managalasi people brought Christianity to the area. There is now a Bible school in the area, training hundreds of people, who are now evangelizing the neighboring areas. Jim passed away in 2019, after a life dedicated to serving the Lord. Jaki has written several books on their work among the Managalasi people and I am happy to call her my friend.*

Trust Your Pilot

(Devotional)

"The LORD himself goes before you and will be with you; he will never leave you nor forsake you. Do not be afraid; do not be discouraged." —Deuteronomy 31:8 (NIV)

The clouds looked like fluffy piles of mashed potatoes covering the Owen-Stanley Mountain range of Papua New Guinea, and we flew directly into them. Usually mission pilots fly in the morning to avoid the build-up of clouds on the mountains every afternoon, but today our flight got a late start. My husband and I, along with our two-year-old son and another couple, were flying to the capital, Port Moresby, on a twin-engine mission plane. The next day we were booked on an international flight to go home for furlough.

I had flown on small planes many times previously, but flying through clouds was a new experience for me. Small planes are not built to fly at higher altitudes where the air is thin, so we could not fly above them.

I noticed the pilot, Will, had some kind of a map balanced on his lap, so I leaned forward. "What are you looking at, Will?" I asked.

"These are mountain chains, and we are flying in the valley between them," said Will. "You notice that some mountain chains dead end—like this one." He pointed to the map. "There's a mountain blocking the end of that valley, with no way out. That's what we need to avoid."

A shudder went through me, my muscles tensing. *What if we're in the wrong valley, one with a mountain at the end?* I thought about it for a while, and then I settled back in my seat. After all, Will was an experienced pilot who had flown this route many times before. I could trust him. I also prayed to the Pilot who guides us with His unseen Hand.

So often in life, our journey is clouded—not with white, fluffy clouds, but the dark, menacing kind that mean a storm is brewing. We can't see the path ahead. Doubt assails us. Maybe the report from the doctor was bad news—the cancer is back. Maybe it's a phone call that our teenager has been in an accident. Or we just found out that our spouse doesn't love us anymore. The baby so awaited has a birth defect and might not live. Or we just lost our job. The list goes on and on.

When the journey ahead terrifies us, we have a God we can trust. God goes with us every step of the way.

Father, help us to trust You fully as we journey into the unknown. You are already holding our future in Your Hands and know what lies ahead. You've told us many times to "fear not." You are leading us and will never leave us or forsake us. Thank You for Your presence in our lives. Amen.

Papua New Guinea. 1981.

Cheering for Chuck

Laughter rang out as children raced across the schoolyard, busily engaged in one of their inventive games. The October wind swirled red and yellow leaves against the brick four-room country school, which had stood like a sentinel on the corner for generations. In 1953, school games were innocent, and the worst school crimes were gum chewing and whispering—and on rare occasions, looking at a neighbor's paper.

"You can't play," said LeRoy, a fourth grader.

"Why not?" I questioned, feeling hurt.

"Because you're only in second grade, and second graders aren't old enough. That's why." He peered at me through thick glasses.

"It's not fair," I protested, turning and walking away.

The game? Catch-the-girls-so-Chucky-can–kiss-them. Chucky was our teacher's fourth grade son, who attended town school. However, today was a teachers' convention at his school. Much to our delight, he visited our school.

Hidden from the playground supervisor's view, the fourth grade boys brought the giggling girls to Chucky.

Several years later, I attended the same town school and church as Chucky. I was acutely aware of his presence in our fourth-sixth grade Sunday school class, but he never even noticed me. Never.

Throughout junior high and high school, Chuck, as he was now called, was popular—handsome, polite, neatly dressed and a good student. I admired him from afar as did other girls. He was out of my league.

Days turned into months and months into years. I graduated from high school, got my university degree and eventually married. Then my husband and I moved overseas.

My mother wrote weekly with local and family news. On rare occasions she mentioned Chuck, who was married and teaching school.

Then a decade later, my mother sent a newspaper clipping. "I know you remember Chuck, so I thought you would like to read what he wrote for the local paper," she wrote. "He's brave to write so openly."

I could hardly believe what I was reading.

"No one understands the pain of mental illness except someone who has lived through it," Chuck wrote. "I am sharing my story to encourage struggling people to get help as I did."

He had lost his wife to divorce, lost his job, and lost his self-respect in a nightmare of mental turmoil. Only when the condition was diagnosed as manic depression and his doctor put him on lithium was he able to find his way out of his mental fog. Now he was finding hope for the future, step by step.

Emotional pain flooded through me as I remembered the Chuck I had known. He had so much potential. He deserved so much better than this! "Lord, be with Chuck," I prayed. "Help him overcome his mental illness."

After that, my path crossed Chuck's every few years. When Chuck's father died, I sent his mother a sympathy card and began writing to her. It was a natural connection since she had once been my teacher.

One time, while writing to her, I shared the playground story from 1953 that I still vividly remembered. It partly belonged to Chuck, and I knew she would pass it on to him. It was my way of saying, "Chuck, I care what happens to you. I always have."

Two summers ago, while my husband, Dennis, and I were visiting the church in my hometown, I saw Chuck. Now in his mid-50s, he was dressed in a multicolored vest buttoned down the front—without a shirt—and had on jeans and sandals. With his longish, wavy hair and beard, he reminded me of a modern-day John the Baptist.

After church, he greeted me with, "I heard you once had a crush on me." He was pleased and gave me a hug. I was glad his mother had passed on the message.

Then he asked, "Did you know that my mother recently

had a stroke? I live at home with her because she needs help. I know she would like company."

"I'm sorry to hear that. I haven't seen her for about five years," I responded.

Dennis and I followed Chuck to his mother's house that was six blocks away. Although the stroke had affected her mobility, she was still alert and remembered me.

After a pleasant visit with his mother, Chuck, Dennis and I talked in the living room. "I miss not having a family of my own," said Chuck wistfully. "You are so fortunate to have each other and your two children."

"God has blessed us," I agreed. "How about you? What are you doing now days?"

"I want to go to Bible school so I can work with street people. The need out there is great," he said with conviction. "I always thought I was a Christian, but three years ago a chaplain who works with street people explained to me what it meant to be a Christian. It's made a big difference in my life. That's why I want to help others who feel hopeless."

"That's great," I said. "I hope things work out for you."

We discussed the challenge going back to school would present. He was dealing with a life-long illness and didn't yet have funding.

When it was time to leave, we wished him well.

"Don't let your dream die," I urged.

Then, on impulse, Chuck picked up a ceramic angel from a coffee table, and held it out to me. "This is for you," he said with a smile. "God bless you both."

Chuck, wherever your path in life takes you, I'll be cheering for you. I always have. I always will.

© 2002 Minnesota
In a phone call to Chuck's mother in 2003, I learned that Multiple Sclerosis has now robbed Chuck of his ability to walk, and the doctors were having difficulty balancing his

medication for his bipolar mood disorder (manic depression). Chuck won't have the opportunity to realize his dream, but there are thousands of other Chucks in the world. Cheer for them and encourage them. The Lord will bless you for it. (Chuck's mother passed away in 2004 and Chuck passed away a number of years later.)

Comfort from Above

Haze hung like a thin gray blanket over Manila. Although it was only 6:30 a.m., I knew the day would be another hot, humid one—my blouse was already sticking to me. Dreading the trip ahead of me, I wished I could make the nightmare of the past few days vanish.

Weaving in and out of traffic, our Filipino driver was taking my co-worker, Helena, and me to the bus station. The traffic was as unnerving to me now as it had been when our family arrived in the Philippines five months earlier to do mission work. An occasional honk of a horn indicated a driver was claiming the right of way.

I settled back against the seat, my mind whirling. I hadn't slept well for several nights and my body was running on adrenaline. My husband, Dennis, had spent several days in the modern Manila Heart Hospital, undergoing tests for the shortness of breath and chest pains he was experiencing. Doctors discovered that his previous heart damage from rheumatic fever had now doubled.

The cardiologist's words ran through my mind like a continuous tape loop: Atrial fibrillation. Sixty percent leakage past the mitral valve. Congestive heart failure. Fluid in the lungs. A dangerously enlarged heart.

The cardiologist told Dennis he needed surgery within a month, or he would face certain death. Even then she didn't know if the surgery would be successful because the damage was so bad. She offered no promises, gave no guarantees.

Today's bus trip would take me back to the little barrio (community) of Lantap, 180 miles north of Manila, where we had been living for the past five weeks. We had been learning one of the national languages. I needed to pack up all of the belongings we had left behind when we hurriedly came to Manila for Dennis' heart tests. My thoughts drifted to Dennis, my husband of 10 years, and our two children who were staying in the mission guesthouse in Manila while I was making my three-day trip.

"Lord, be with them today; keep them safe," I prayed silently. Over the past few days I had looked at dozens of Bible verses on peace and comfort. I had been praying constantly, but God's peace still eluded me. My one question was: would I be a widow at 39?

"Lord, I know You want me to trust You, but I'm finding it hard. You'll have to help me. I'm so afraid."

"I recognize that corner," said Helena, seated next to me. Her words jolted me back to the present. "The bus station will be on our right in about three blocks."

Since we were early, we had our choice of seats on the bus. The 180-mile trip ahead of us through the mountains would take between seven and nine hours with many stops along the way. I closed my eyes, feeling exhausted. I was trying so hard to trust God, but the anxious thoughts kept crowding my mind.

Other passengers were now beginning to fill the bus. I looked up just as two young men entered. One was carrying a guitar and both had lapel pins. As they came closer, I could see one pin read "Trust God" and the other was a cross within a fish. Were they Christians?

Finding seats directly in front of us, the two men turned around to greet us. They knew English well. "Are the two of you with SIL?" asked the younger man.

"Yes. How did you know?" I gasped, shocked that we could be so easily identified in a city of 10 million people. How had they heard of SIL, the Bible translation organization with which Helena and I were working?

"You don't look like tourists because you don't have a camera around your neck," was their response. "You're not dressed like tourists."

The Filipino man of Chinese descent explained he was Pastor Lim from a small church about 40 miles beyond where we were going. He said he had met someone from SIL on his previous travels.

Pastor Lim's traveling companion introduced himself as Rogel. He said he worked with a mission in Banaue.

Helena settled back in her seat with a magazine, while I continued my conversation with Pastor Lim. He talked about how he was the first in his Buddhist family to become a Christian, and how the rest of his family rejected him and his choice of occupation.

I told him that I had a husband and two children who were staying in the mission guesthouse in Manila.

"If you have a family, why are you traveling alone?" he asked.

"My husband has a serious heart condition. I need to go back and pack up our things." Conversation with this gentle man came easily. "God wants me to trust Him, but I'm afraid my husband might die," I said, wiping tears from my eyes with a tissue.

"God loves you very much and is watching over your family," Pastor Lim replied with certainty. "Your husband will be all right." For the next hour Pastor Lim turned around in his seat and lovingly shared Scripture and God's comfort with me. Then he prayed with me.

God's peace, which had been eluding me, flooded over me. I felt His presence in this encounter with this stranger in a way I never had before. "Thanks Lord, for showing me you care for me. Now I trust You."

As I thought about this incident shortly afterward, questions raced through my mind. Just who were these two men? How had they chosen seats directly in front of us? How did they know who we were? A Bible verse from Hebrews then came to mind. "Do not forget to entertain strangers, for by so doing some people have entertained angels without knowing it" (Hebrews 13:2 NIV).

When I reached the bamboo house in Lantap, I packed everything we owned back into the crate we had brought from the U.S. Then I returned to Manila by bus three days later. Because Dennis's survival was uncertain, we decided to go back to the United States for the surgery. There we would be surrounded by our families.

Heart damage in the U.S. was rated 1 to 4, with 4 being the most serious. Doctors ranked Dennis as 4 plus. However, true to Pastor Lim's prediction, Dennis came through the surgery well. The mechanical valve that clicks in his chest is still working 35 years later.

In the years that have passed since our time in the Philippines in 1985, I've often thought about the incident on the bus. Were the strangers who they said they were . . . or had I entertained angels? The strangers seemed as human as I am, but who understands God's ways? Of one thing I am certain—it was a God-arranged encounter. My two "angels" came with God's message of love and comfort when I desperately needed it.

1985, Philippines. This story floated around the Internet for years and encouraged many people who emailed me.

Exactly the Right Teacher

Autumn leaves drifted down on a sunny Saturday morning in late October 1985. I stood watching our children through a sliding glass door in the house where we were temporarily staying. Rachel, three, was rolling in the thick layer of leaves on the ground, while Tim, six, was busily making piles with a rake which was much too big for him. Noticing me standing there, Tim came over to the door.

"Mom, did you see the big pile of leaves I made?" he asked, a grin spreading across his face.

"Yes, I've been watching you," I said. "You're doing a great job." I was glad to see the two of them playing and acting like normal children. All the changes they had been through in the past three weeks had taken their toll, making Tim and Rachel into confused, fearful children. The changes had taken an emotional toll on me too.

Three weeks earlier my critically ill husband, Dennis, our two children and I had boarded a plane in the Philippines where we were doing mission work. Now we were half a world away in Minnesota. Tim, Rachel, and I had stayed with various family members while my husband was hospitalized for open heart surgery. Living out of two suitcases—all the worldly possessions we had with us—left us feeling uprooted.

A mechanical heart valve now clicked loudly in Dennis' chest. Diagnosed with congestive heart failure and given just a few weeks to live, he now had a new lease on life through the surgery.

Throughout the ordeal we saw God's provision for us in unexpected ways. This house where our children were now happily playing in the leaves was one of these provisions. Del and Louise, a couple from our church whom we knew slightly, had graciously offered our family a place to stay for the first 10 days after Dennis was out of the hospital. After our time with them, we would be moving into a house-sitting situation in another suburb.

Del and Louise's house was in a Minneapolis suburb where we knew no one—a fact which made what happened next all the more remarkable.

A former teacher, Louise was concerned that Tim was missing school. After being away from school for three weeks, he showed little interest in working on the reading and math workbooks I brought with me.

"Tim really needs some structure to his days," Louise told me. "I know the principal at the local elementary school and I've arranged for Tim to go to class there on Monday."

"Do you think that's a good idea for such a short time?" I asked. "After all, we'll soon be moving and he'll be attending a different school."

Louise assured me that being in school was the best place for Tim and I reluctantly agreed.

Later, as I thought over the plan to put Tim in school, I wondered how Tim would fit in. Would it be another traumatic experience for him? I had taught school previously and knew it could be difficult for a teacher to take a new student in for a short time. Other students already had a familiar routine. Would the teacher feel resentful having a student for only a few days? Would he be accepted by the other children?

When I told Tim about the plan for him to go to school on Monday, he was not thrilled by the prospect.

"Mommy, I don't want to go to school," he pleaded, fear showing in his brown eyes. "I want to stay here with you."

That night I wrestled with the issue. "Lord, show me that I'm doing the right thing in sending Tim to school," I prayed. "He's scared and has been through so many changes already."

On Monday morning Tim reluctantly got ready for school. After breakfast, Dennis stiffly moved to a comfortable chair to do some reading. Since he was unable to watch an active three year old, Rachel came with us.

The autumn air felt crisp as Tim, Rachel and I got into

the car with Louise who drove us to the nearby school. After this first day, Tim would be able to ride a bus to get there.

Louise introduced me to the principal. Then she stood by the office holding Rachel's hand—to keep her from following us—while the principal, Tim and I walked down the hall to the first grade classroom.

"Miss Nibbe is good with children," the principal assured me, tapping lightly on the door. "I'm sure she'll make Tim feel right at home. I already arranged with her for Tim to join her class."

A pleasant woman about my age opened the door. After the principal introduced us to her as "Tim and his mother, Mrs. Seever," Miss Nibbe turned to me. "I know you," she said. "You're Jan."

I was stunned. "How did you know?" I gasped.

The principal looked dumbfounded.

"Your husband used to be active in our singles' Bible study group about 10 years ago," explained Miss Nibbe. "The group still meets. When a couple of our group members heard Dennis was critically ill in the Philippines, we all started praying for him. We've been praying for your family since that time."

Then she turned to her class, "I want you to meet Tim who has been living in a country which is far away. The country is called the Philippines. Please welcome Tim."

"Andy, Joel and Christy," she said to several students near the front of the room, "please show Tim the art project you're working on."

Tim was already happily absorbed in activity by the time I left.

As the principal and I walked down the hallway, he turned to me. "How did she know who you were?" He repeated the question several times, not quite believing what he heard.

On the ride back to the house with Louise, I started thinking about a get well card Dennis had received from the Bible study group. I knew about half of the people who signed the card. Other names weren't familiar to me.

When I got to the house, I found the card. Sure enough. One of the people who had signed that card was Marilyn Nibbe. And yes, Dennis did remember her as someone he knew from the group.

"Thanks, Lord," I later prayed, "for showing me that you were taking care of us all the time. Thanks for providing a teacher who understood Tim's needs perfectly."

1985 Minnesota. I had an opportunity to be in touch with Marilyn Nibbe several times—as recently as Fall 2018.

God's Handprints

We saw God's provision in the "angels" who rode with me on the trip back up to Lantap ("Comfort from Above") and later for the provision of a teacher who understood our son's situation and had already been praying for our family ("Exactly the Right Teacher"). There were other things, too, that we couldn't explain and were evidence of God's provision

After I packed all of our possessions back into our shipping crate, I made the trip back to the guesthouse in Manila alone and rejoined the rest of my family. On the advice of our doctor, we finally decided to return to the U.S. in case the surgery was unsuccessful and Dennis died. We began making travel and surgery arrangements by phone Then one night at supper in the mission guesthouse, a couple staying there handed us a slip of paper with the telephone number of Dr. Famorca, the brother-in-law of our landlady and owner of the bamboo house in which we had been living.

The couple, Bible translators, had been visiting their hospitalized Filipino co-worker, and Dr. Famorca was the attending physician. When Dr. Famorca asked them what they, as Americans, were doing in the Philippines, they told him they were doing Bible translation. "Do you know the Seevers?" asked Dr. Famorca. "I need to find out if they plan to live in my house again, and I don't know how to reach them." We were able to use the phone number they handed us and talk with Dr. Famorca. Just a coincidence? Hardly, in a city of 10 million people.

While in the hospital waiting room during surgery in Minneapolis, I felt God's comfort and sensed people praying for us. During the surgery, doctors replaced Dennis' badly damaged mitral valve with a St. Jude mechanical valve, again a provision from the Lord. (The Filipino doctors had planned to use a pig-skin valve which calcifies and needs replacement in five to seven years; their second choice — a Bjork-Shyli mechanical valve — was later found to have a high failure rate and has since been recalled.)

When Dennis was released from the hospital, we stayed temporarily with friends (See "Exactly the Right Teacher.")

The Lord provided for us in many other amazing ways as well—a rent-free house-sitting opportunity for four months, a good hospital for me when I developed pancreatitis and needed gall bladder surgery three weeks after Dennis' surgery, and my mother's availability to assist our family—due to a couple unusual circumstances—when Dennis and I were both healing from our surgeries.

All of this happened many years ago, but at times when I get fearful or discouraged, I remember those five weeks in 1985 in awe when I saw God's "handprints" so dramatically on our lives. I serve a God who sends "angels" to minister to me, knows me by name and can track me down among 10 million people.

1985 Philippines. A longer version of this was published in an InScribe Christian Writers' Fellowship publication.

Comfort in Times of Trouble
(Devotional)

Praise be to the God and Father of our Lord Jesus Christ, the Father of compassion and the God of all comfort, who comforts us in all our troubles, so that we can comfort those in any trouble with the comfort we ourselves receive from God (2 Corinthians 1:3-4 NIV).

"I'm so glad your husband is coming to the retreat," wrote Doris in her email. "It means that I won't be the only one there with mobility issues." Her words surprised me at first, but then I understood.

My husband suffered a major stroke in 2004, and along with the loss of speech, he now walks slowly with a cane. A life-changing event for both of us, the stroke suddenly threw me into the role of caregiver and turned our world upside down.

At the conference, Doris and I greeted each other warmly. I knew her from one face-to-face conversation, but mostly from short emails, since she lives in another province. In her early 50s, she now uses a walker because of a mysterious, undiagnosed illness that is gradually stealing her motor skills. Her life has undergone a dramatic change in the past few years.

"People just don't understand," she confided, as she freely shared with me at coffee break some of the challenges she and her family are facing. She instinctively knew I *would* understand, and I did. There was an automatic bond between us. And I was able to tell her how the Lord has been faithful throughout the years in spite of numerous difficulties our family has been through.

Later, I reflected on the retreat with Laura, a friend of mine. "When I look back, I think the most valuable thing I have to offer others has come through the difficulties the Lord has brought me through—especially my husband's stroke and the bipolar mood disorder in our family," I told her. "Those very things that were so painful at the time are what the Lord has used to enable me to relate to and comfort other people."

Laura was intrigued.

I went on to explain how when my husband first had his stroke, a friend told me, "What a tragedy." I thought about it for a while, and said to myself, "I'd rather see it as a challenge." A tragedy looks back at what used to be, but a challenge looks forward to the future, giving a person a reason to hold on to hope.

And challenges we certainly have had, but the Lord has never abandoned us. He has given me joy for the journey, and His peace and presence. And for that, I thank Him. He has also enabled me to be a comfort to others going through struggles.

Thank you, Lord, for comforting each of us in times of trouble, that we might be a comfort to others when they are going through difficult times. Amen.

Learning Lasts a Lifetime

It was a warm June night in Dallas, Texas, in 1983. Several dozen people, laughing and chatting, had gathered in a backyard for a pot luck dinner for missionaries who serve with Wycliffe Bible Translators in Papua New Guinea, where my husband Dennis and I had recently completed a four-year term. As I looked around the group, I recognized everyone except one person—a tall middle-aged man with a camera slung around his neck.

I introduced myself, and discovered he was Hugh Steven, here at the pot luck to gather stories for a missions book he was writing.

I was in awe! This man had written numerous books about Wycliffe, and I had read many of them.

I thought quickly. "I've just written a story and wonder if you could look at it," I said.

His response at first was unenthusiastic. No doubt it was a request he had gotten many times, far too many.

"It's a story about a girl we met when we traveled home for furlough from Papua New Guinea," I continued, as fast as I could, afraid he would lose interest. "In 1981, my husband, our infant son and I traveled to Canton, China, as part of a tour group and met a 19-year-old young woman on a street corner. She wanted to practice her English, so we gave her a bilingual Gospel of Mark, and she later became a Christian through reading it."

Now he was interested.

Mr. Steven read my story the next day while I sat beside him, nervously waiting. I was still in awe that I was sitting in the same room with this man whom I greatly admired. Was it really happening?

"This is good," he said. "Very good." As he read through each page, he marked it here and there with his red pen. "You have potential. Get some training."

He told me to send the story to *Power for Living*, an adult Sunday school paper used across the U.S. and Canada. He had had many articles published there and knew the editor personally.

"In your cover letter, you can mention that I read it and suggested you send it to them," he said, handing my manuscript back to me. Wow! What a gift to an inexperienced writer! What a gift to *any* writer.

The story, "Hello, My Name is Aileen,"—the first story I ever submitted—was published, and I was hooked! I wanted to share my writing with the world and make a difference.

Following Mr. Steven's suggestion, I took a two-year correspondence course called "Discover Your Possibilities in Writing," taught by Norman Rohrer, through the Christian Writers' Guild located in California. I began the course with two children at home: four-year-old Timothy and 18-month-old Rachel—while I was living in Dallas and working half time in the Wycliffe bookstore at the International Linguistics Center, which offers academic training for missionaries. Between working, caring for my family, and completing the assignments, I hardly had time to breathe. However, I was happy and fulfilled, sensing that writing was part of God's plan for my life. I enjoyed the challenge!

Our work in missions meant we traveled a lot, sometimes quite unexpectedly. I carried the course work with me from Dallas to the Philippines, and then back to the United States and to Australia. It took me longer than the expected two years to complete the course, but my instructor was patient. During that time, while in the Philippines, Dennis nearly died of a heart problem that required immediate open heart surgery to replace a badly damaged mitral valve. We traveled to Minnesota for his surgery. At that time, I was trying to hold my family together with all of the moves, plus dealing with disoriented young children. Then, three weeks after Dennis' surgery, I was in the hospital with pancreatitis and needed gall bladder surgery. Fortunately, my mother was able to help with both of us patients and our children, but my writing came to a halt. However, after I recovered, I plowed through the course, not giving up. At the completion of the course after three years, I had an article published in *Decision* magazine, sharing the amazing testimony of friends who both became Christians after the birth of their son, who had spina bifida.

Did I have any idea earlier that I wanted to write? When I was in high school, the adviser to our school newspaper asked me if I wanted to write for the newspaper because he had noticed my writing skills. Surprised to be asked, I was delighted to join the writing team. At first I was a reporter, then assistant editor and finally in Grade 12, I was the editor. In university, I took a year of Honours English, partly focusing on writing and partly on literature. Mr. Regnier, the best university instructor I ever had, expanded our world view and challenged us daily for that whole first year. I was a country girl from a small town, so this was a new experience for me. However, after a grueling second year of English literature classes—with less than memorable instructors— I decided to major in biology education instead. That was the end of English for me, or so I thought.

Then, nearly two decades later in 1982-1983, I was working in the Wycliffe bookstore at the International Linguistics Center. As I looked through the missions books and academic books on the shelves, I kept thinking, *I could write, I could do that. I have writing skills.* That original spark for writing was *not* dead. It was a glowing ember, waiting to be fanned. My encounter with Mr. Steven brought the hidden desire to write to life.

When embarking on my writing journey in 1983, I started collecting books on writing. *Writing to Inspire* by William Gentz and Lee Roddy, the first book in my collection became my favorite. I was encouraged to learn that God could use my stories to make a difference in the lives of others. I also subscribed to a Christian writing magazine, which gave me numerous writing ideas and helped me understand how the writing market worked. The magazine also had articles about Christian writers whom I admired and how they got started writing. I was inspired to become a writer!

I discovered that writers need to be readers too. William Faulkner said: "Read, read, read….and see how (authors) do it. Just like a carpenter who works as an apprentice and studies the master. Read! You'll absorb it. Then write. If it's good, you'll find out. If it's not, throw it out of the window."

Growing Strong in the Seasons of Life, by Charles Swindoll, taught me the art of using short anecdotes to show biblical truths; various books by Max Lucado showed me that good writing can sound as natural as speaking. I learned about the art of engaging fiction from L.M. Montgomery, whose Anne of Green Gables series is classic, and C.S. Lewis inspired me with his profound wisdom. But the Bible tops the list, because I know its Author.

Writing also takes practice, practice, and more practice. If a person is learning along the way, writing improves. Otherwise the same mistakes are repeated over and over again. At first I liberally sprinkled my writing with adjectives and adverbs, but I soon discovered that too many is a mark of a beginner. Mark Twain said, "If you see an adverb, kill it." True! Words that end in 'ly' are no longer my close friends; the trick was to find much stronger verbs and nouns. I also tracked down the passive voice and substituted the active voice.

Learning to write natural-sounding dialogue comes from being a good listener. People don't speak in long paragraphs and often interrupt each other. I learned that dialogue should be tagged with "he said" and "she said," rather than words that call attention to themselves like "she postulated." Good writing can pair an action with dialogue so tags aren't even needed. For instance: "That's not what we agreed on! You have no right to change it without asking me!" Kelly wadded up the offending paper and fired it at the wastepaper basket, missing by a mile.

I also worked on showing and not telling, something that I'm still learning. Telling comes naturally to most writers, but showing takes much more thought and effort. Telling only establishes facts, but showing adds life to a person's writing and invites the reader to hear, feel, taste, touch and see. It engages all of the reader's senses.

Joining InScribe in 1998 put a spark into my writing and brought encouragement from other writers. Conferences like the Fall Conference and the Spring WorDshop put me in touch with seasoned writers over the years. The ones who encouraged me the most were Luci Shaw, Deborah Gyapong and Kathleen Gibson. In 1998, I was just getting started writing again after a time of deep discouragement because of a number of family health problems. Luci Shaw, who had written an article dealing with a painful season of life, took the time to talk with me on a personal level. How encouraging that was! Deborah Gyapong told a powerful personal story of how just *one book* she read—while she was in a state of rebellion—led her to the Lord and changed her entire life. This encouraged me to persevere in my writing, for my words could be life-changing. Kathleen Gibson shared how, from a small beginning, her writing was published by *Reader's Digest*—an amazing success story. She is a master of showing, not telling. After each conference, I carried inspiration home and read through my pages of notes, ready to tackle the next challenge. Yes, I am a writer!

All of this encouragement, background and training has helped me in my writing. I've written articles that have appeared in magazines, newspapers, online and in gift books, and for the past seven years I've written articles for a megachurch newspaper, telling people's amazing testimonies. Many times I've gotten positive responses from readers who have been encouraged.

The main writing I do now is through Wycliffe Bible Translators where I am the editor of the prayer magazine *Prayer Alive*, a writer and a proof reader. While my writing and editing for the *Prayer Alive* may not be "stories" or exciting in the same sense as my other writing, I'm extending God's work by sharing news and prayer requests with Wycliffe's 2,000 or so prayer partners. *Prayer Alive* is also available online.

Recently, my writing came full circle when I received an e-mail from a woman, who wrote, ". . . Prayer is one ministry us oldies can have. We joined Wycliffe in 1956. We're now 83 but up until about three years ago, [my husband] was still writing Wycliffe books. . . . I just wanted to tell you that I so enjoyed meeting the Wycliffe members and praying for them this month [through *Prayer Alive*]. . . . Thank you for your good editing and making the requests known. . . ."

The woman who wrote that e-mail is Norma Steven, the wife of Hugh Steven, the man who got me started in writing!

Calgary, 2015. This was published in 7 Essential Habits of Christian Writers, *a book produced by InScribe Christian Writers' Fellowship.*

Our Gentle Little Friend

"Mom, I really want a cat. Please? I'll take care of it." Twelve-year-old Rachel's insistent plea came often.

My reply was always the same. "We don't stay anywhere long enough to have a pet. Remember how sad you were when we gave away Midnight and Princess?"

My husband and I moved a lot with our jobs and had given our cats to friends when moving from Australia and from Dallas, Texas.

After saying "no" many times, I finally said, "How about something smaller like a hamster?"

Rachel had seen teddy bear hamsters in the pet store, and the idea of owning one of these cuddly creatures delighted her. She talked of nothing else the whole week.

Finally, on Saturday we went to a pet store. She was in heaven! She visited all of the kittens, puppies, mice, gerbils and parakeets. When we finally got to the teddy bear hamster cage, a store employee came over to help us.

"These are all young males," he said, reaching into the cage to take out a hamster. Rachel chose a white one banded with brown. It was love at first sight.

Of course one never buys just a hamster. The cage and all the equipment cost a small fortune, but it was worth it if it made Rachel happy and kept her from constantly asking for a cat.

Rachel's hero was Abraham Lincoln so she named the hamster Abraham.

Abraham was shy at first, but soon got used to Rachel, who carried him around inside her shirt and gave him free rein in her room.

About a week later, Rachel came to me. "I'm worried about Abraham. He's hiding inside of his nest of tissues in the corner and hasn't been out all day. I wonder if he's sick or something."

After trying to rouse Abraham, she suddenly shrieked. "What are all of these little pink things?" Abraham bared his teeth and hissed at her.

As I peered into the cage, I discovered seven naked babies. So Abraham wasn't really Abraham after all. He was a she and soon was renamed Abby.

As the babies grew up, Rachel discovered she could put an ad in a local "bargain finder" and sell them at eight dollars each. Abby helped her make some spending money. We later purchased a male and Abby produced three more litters. A number of our friends ended up with Abby's offspring.

At that point it appeared we wouldn't be moving, so Rachel persuaded us to get a cat which she named Belle. Sometimes Abby would chase a terrified Belle with her exercise ball, rolling after the cat. Other times when they were both out, Belle would jump over Abby and bat at her gently with her paw. It was a game. They didn't know they were supposed to be natural enemies. Rachel sometimes put Abby on Belle's back, and Belle tolerated it. On occasion she would leave the two of them together loose in her room for hours. Belle never harmed Abby.

One day in 1997 when Abby was three—old age for a hamster—she was in her exercise ball. No one realized the door to the basement was open, and Abby bounced her way down the stairs. It was actually her second unscheduled trip down those stairs, but this time it was too much for our gentle friend. She died a few days later. Rachel cried for a long time and the rest of us grieved as well.

But Abby was not to be forgotten. I found evidence of her long afterward, like the time I pulled open the bottom desk drawer and found chewed photos and envelopes. So that's where she hid when she was lost. I later found Abby droppings when I cleaned a closet. I still have curtains with tiny holes nibbled in one place when Abby's cage was too close.

Abby prints are here and there, but there's one place where they will indelibly remain. During her short sojourn in life, this gentle little friend made an imprint on our hearts.

1995 Calgary

I Choose to Laugh

The ringing phone woke me out of a sound sleep at 11:35 p.m. I fumbled to reach it beside my bed.

"Hello," I mumbled.

"Mom, I'm not in jail," said my 21-year-old daughter, Rachel. "What?" I was groggy, but my heart was beginning to race.

"I'm not actually. I'm fine. It's my car."

"What's the matter?"

"My car was impounded. I just found out that since it's registered in your name, you have to be the one to get it out."

I knew earlier in the day that her rust-bucket of a car had been towed and she had been trying to locate it. She found it at the city car impoundment lot—which closed at midnight. It was in the industrial area of the city of 900,000. I wasn't at all familiar with that part of the city, so I avoided it even in daylight.

I woke my hard-of-hearing husband, who had missed the ringing phone, and explained the situation. Fortunately, his concern for his daughter outweighed his anger at being awakened. The two of us drove down the darkened streets together.

"I hope someday that she will believe what she reads," I said wistfully. "This morning she parked in the half-empty parking lot of an apartment building when she stopped to visit a friend. She ignored the sign that said 'unauthorized vehicles will be towed at the owner's expense.'" (She had collected parking tickets previously by parking in unauthorized places because of over-crowding in college parking lots, but this was her first towing experience.)

When we arrived at the lot, Rachel and her chauffeur friend were waiting for us. They were in such a good mood that she got me laughing too. The woman at the desk stared at us in disbelief. No doubt she had seen a good many confrontations between parents and children in similar situations.

"I expected you to be really upset," I said to my daughter.

"It was a choice between crying and laughing," Rachel said. "I choose to laugh."

Why had she waited so long to go to the impoundment lot? She answered that she had watched her favorite TV program at 10 p.m. to unwind after getting off work at 8 p.m.

As my husband and I drove home, a little short of sleep, I thought of other parents who get phone calls in the night from their children—who really are in jail, or from police who inform them that their child was in an accident, or worse.

A "jailed" car was such a minor thing. So many other upsetting situations in life later prove to be minor as well. I, too, choose to laugh.

Calgary, 2002. This was used in a weekly e-mail called "Insight for the Day."

Dark Threads in the Tapestry of Life

"My life is but a weaving between my Lord and me," penned an unknown poet in "The Weaver." The third and fourth verses read:

"Not until the loom is silent/ and the shuttles cease to fly shall God unroll the canvas/and explain the reason why the dark threads are as needful/ in the weaver's skillful hands as the threads of gold and silver/ in the pattern He has planned."

I understand dark threads. I've had many in my life.

No starry-eyed bride imagines her beloved any different than she pictures him as she says, "I do." She cannot see how mental illness can insidiously affect every aspect of life, choking out hope and joy, strangling relationships. No mother lovingly holding her newborn baby can anticipate the turmoil of the teenage years. Yet these things happen.

When Dennis and I married in 1975, our goal was to serve the Lord through Wycliffe Bible Translators and everything went well at first. My goal was to have a happy home and a Christian marriage. Then gradually, puzzling things happened. When Dennis was feeling down, his dark moods often showed up as anger. He thought it was my responsibility to make him happy, and I didn't know how. The "how-to-be-happily-married" variety of books—I read many of them—didn't work. Wasn't I trying hard enough? By this time, we had two children.

In spite of happy and fulfilling times, the moods kept returning. For years Dennis was so good at covering his feelings around his co-workers, that they thought of him as a kind, extremely helpful person. Life was very much like living on a roller coaster.

During those difficult times, I found my solace in the Lord. I poured my heart out into my journal, sometimes writing prayers, sometimes just recording the pain. I felt so alone. At other times my cries to God were wordless. Tears seldom came, but often I felt numb.

By the time we returned from Australia for furlough in 1990, the situation was unbearable. Swallowing my pride, I sought help from the counseling department at the International Linguistics Center in Dallas where the counselors were very supportive. They also recommended a co-dependency support group.

On our sixteenth wedding anniversary, Dennis told me he was leaving me. He expected his family to make him happy, but he just wasn't happy, so we must be his problem. He wanted to get away from us, but was too confused to figure out a way to do it, so it never happened.

One time I remember wanting to stand on a high hill somewhere and scream at the top of my lungs. Not that it would help the situation any, but it was an expression of the unbearable, mind-numbing emotional pain I was feeling.

Getting help for Dennis was another matter. Often those with emotional difficulties are the last to admit they need help. At first he reluctantly went to a few counseling sessions, but quit because they "weren't doing any good." It took eight months and the advice of a number of skilled people before I persuaded Dennis to seek help. A psychiatrist quickly diagnosed depressive disorder in September 1990. An anti-depressant brought relief for many of the symptoms within two weeks. The diagnosis was later changed several times, but the depressive part of the diagnosis still remains.

A few years later our teenage son went through a time of turmoil. Struggling with anger and depression, he tried to drop out of high school several times each year. I was caught in the middle as the peacemaker between a confused, angry son and a depressed husband. I wrote in my journal, "My heart aches—for a son struggling to grow up, for a father who doesn't understand him at all, for a son who hates his father for not understanding him, for a father who hates his son for hating him."

During this time, our teenage daughter seemed to be doing well, but later I found out she had struggles of her own that just weren't apparent at the time.

In the midst of all of this, the Lord brought wonderful, encouraging friends. Sometimes we would talk, at other times my friends would just let me talk while they listened. They always let me know they were praying for me. One special friend, Margaret, would send me a card every few weeks with a caring note inside. She would clip out encouraging poetry that she would put into her cards. I taped every one of those cards into my journal, which became much more like a scrapbook.

"I want so much to lovingly assure you that my husband and I care and we hurt with you," Margaret wrote in one of her cards. "The Lord knows how much we can take and knows our breaking point. You'll surely be refined as gold when you see His answers and until then, keep on trusting Him." What a blessing her encouragement was to me!

The Lord constantly brought reassurances to me through His Word as well. The Bible says, "The Lord is near to the brokenhearted, and saves the crushed in spirit" (Psalms 34:18 NIV) and "When I am afraid I will trust in you" (Psalms 56:3 NIV). It also says that He will never leave us or forsake us: "*The LORD himself goes before you and will be with you; he will never leave you nor forsake you. Do not be afraid; do not be discouraged.*" (Deuteronomy 31:8). The Lord has proved those promises over and over again in my life.

So what has happened to my family over the years? With a lot of prayer and prodding, our son finished high school in 1997. He graduated from a university with high honors, and holds a full-time job. Our daughter also has a university degree and is working full time as well.

My husband was finally diagnosed with bipolar mood disorder in 1997, which explained why my life felt as if I were on a roller coaster. He is doing much better now with a proper balance of medication. It's a lifetime illness, so life will always be challenging. He has always been able to hold a job, for which I am thankful.

Things That Have Been Personally Helpful to Us

What would my advice be for those in a similar situation? The following things have been personally helpful to us in dealing with my husband's illness:

- Be aware of the symptoms and don't pretend everything is "normal" like I did.
- Get help. Trained counselors are available inside and outside of Wycliffe. A family doctor can prescribe medication for a simple case of depression, but it takes a psychiatrist to diagnose the more complicated cases.
- Love unconditionally and be sensitive to your spouse's needs.
- A mood disorder caused by a chemical imbalance is just as real a disease as diabetes and requires professional help and medication.
- The illness may be long-term, requiring medication for the rest of the patient's life as is the case for my husband. Getting help meant a change of assignment for us, and we spent two-and-a-half years in Dallas.
- Finding a network of trusted friends to pray for me and my husband and listen to me has been very helpful. A support group also helps.
- I learned to rely on the Lord in a way I never have before.

One of the most valuable resources I have found in coming to terms with my husband's mood disorder is the book *Why Do Christians Shoot Their Wounded? Helping (Not Hurting) Those with Emotional Difficulties* (InterVarsity Press) by Dr. Dwight L. Carlson, a Christian psychiatrist. He shows in a very helpful chart that as low as the average person feels when depressed, this is only the *beginning point* for someone with a mood disorder. According to Dr. Carlson, telling a person with a chemical imbalance that "Jesus is all you need," and telling them if they were obedient to the Lord, they wouldn't be struggling with depression only heaps more guilt them. It's no sin to hurt.

And what about me? I still journal, but the frantic prayers and deep emotional pain no longer fill the pages. As I look back over the past years, the words "commitment" and "perseverance" have taken on a personal meaning for me in my life and marriage. I thank the Lord for His goodness and what He has brought us through. He has taught me many things and now is allowing me to encourage others who are going through similar difficulties.

The tapestry of life will bring more dark threads in the future, but I know God is with me. He gives me grace for the journey—one day at a time.

2000, Calgary. Dennis had a very large stroke in 2004, and as a result, had seizures a few times a year. He was put on Tegretol to control the seizures, and as a side effect of the medication, his bipolar mood disorder is under much better control than previously. Although Why Do Christians Shoot Their Wounded *was published in 1994, it is still in print and is available through Amazon. I highly recommend it.*

Consider It a Challenge

No one plans for it, wishes for it, or works it into their retirement scheme. But according to U.S. Social Security, three people out of 10 are disabled before they retire. My husband is one of them.

"Doe." He says the word as his blue eyes peer intently into mine.

"No." I repeat the word. "Watch where I put my lips and teeth, Dennis."

"No." This time it sounds much more like what it was meant to be. We repeat it about a dozen times and go on to the next word.

"Why," I say, exaggerating the position of my mouth and he mimics me. We do the next six words, a dozen times each, and then flip the page over and begin on the phrases. We repeat this day after day . . . for months.

In Nov. 2004, a very large stroke reduced my fifty-eight-year-old husband, Dennis, from the independent man he once was to someone dependent on others. He once rode a motorcycle and was an avid reader in his spare time. He often visited several elderly shut-ins and was building a large model railroad layout in our basement. He once was a skilled maintenance worker and had training in accounting.

The stroke affected the right parietal, temporal and frontal areas of the brain, and left him totally paralyzed on his right side for the next six weeks. His speech was gone. My son, daughter and I were delighted on Christmas Day when he was able to move his fingers on his right hand—it was our "Christmas miracle."

Dennis learned to spell his own name on a children's plastic spelling board with buttons he could press for each letter. His speech therapists worked with him on spelling his name, of course, but my daughter and I used that spelling board with him day after day until the spelling was correct. DENNIS wasn't as difficult to spell as SEEVER. At first it was DEEVER, REEVER, DEEVES or REEVES. When he finally got it consistently right, we all rejoiced.

Strokes are life-changing events for the entire family. Not only did that stroke dramatically change my husband's life, but my world was turned upside down as well. During the first months, I felt numb and had difficulty thinking. For months afterward, my world centered on my husband and his needs.

When I asked what the prognosis was, one doctor told me, "I expect that your husband will walk again some day, but because the area affected was so large, your husband will probably be quite handicapped, especially in the area of speech."

No! That wasn't what I wanted to hear at all. That wasn't the future I wanted to face! So I asked, "Do patients ever surprise you?" to which he responded, "All the time." That gave me the hope I needed—like a flickering candle in a dark room. "Let Dennis be one of those stroke patients who surprises him," was my prayer.

Within the first couple months after it happened, a friend of mine referred to Dennis' stroke as a tragedy. I'm sure most people would think of strokes as tragedies. I thought about it for a while and concluded I would rather see it as a major *challenge* in our lives. "Tragedy" looks backward at all he has lost, and he has lost so much. However, "challenge" looks forward to what Dennis can regain if he works hard enough at it. "Tragedy" speaks of defeat, but "challenge" focuses on hope for the future. That hope was what we desperately needed to keep pressing forward.

During those long, difficult months I held onto a Bible verse about hope, and a song with words of hope about God's faithfulness in the midst of life's storms. My faith kept me from being dashed against the rocks in this raging storm of life when nothing made sense.

Following his stroke, Dennis worked hard for 16 months in three different rehabilitation hospitals. For the last nine months, he lived in the Brain Injury Unit of a hospital 120 miles away from home. Only a few people were chosen for this state-of-the-art rehabilitation hospital, based on their age (under 65), willingness to work hard, and potential for progress. I was deeply grateful that he was chosen.

I made those long trips back and forth to visit him on weekends or would occasionally bring him home for a long weekend. At times I encountered white-knuckle driving—dense fog, slippery roads or blinding snow.

When the weather was good, I put my favorite music CD in the CD player, and sang along as the miles slipped by. Singing was a great stress reliever. As the seasons changed, I watched changes in the Canadian countryside around me week by week—the new leaves on the trees, growing fields of wheat and canola, golden leaves of autumn, hoarfrost on trees in the winter. When the traffic was light, it was a time of solitude.

Progress was slow, but Dennis worked as hard as he could. By March 2006, however, it became apparent that he was ready to leave, much as a child loses interest in working hard as the end of school approaches.

Dennis finally moved home on March 6, 2006, and I became his caregiver. Prior to Dennis' stroke this was not a role I had ever imagined myself in. I could see myself as a widow as the autumn of life approached, but as a caregiver? Never. I learned quickly.

Today Dennis walks well with a cane, but has little use of his right hand and arm.

True to the doctor's prediction, he has regained very little speech, which is limited to a couple dozen words (spontaneous speech that is located in another part of the brain). He struggles with both aphasia and apraxia. However, he is able to sing the song "Happy Birthday", because singing is located in a different part of the brain. He hums along with familiar hymns in church.

Lack of reading and writing skills also remains a major roadblock to communication. He can recognize words that are meaningful to him—auction, propane powered truck, model railroad, 4 x 4, sports, and football. He is also able to locate a football game on TV using the TV guide. He can write his name from memory, but nothing else. He communicates with me through gestures or by drawing pictures. We're slowly developing our own greatly simplified version of sign language.

I'm fortunate that I was able to continue working at my job, and that I now work on projects that can be done, in part, while working at my computer at home. I am also fortunate that our adult son and daughter help me out on occasion and we have a multitude of friends who pray for us regularly.

At first he was on a long waiting list, but Dennis is now involved in a number of community programs for the handicapped. These programs have been a major step in giving him back some semblance of a life. His depression has lifted as he realizes there are still things he can do, places he can go, and people he can interact with. He is also beginning to realize that he's not the only person with a handicap.

One time he brought an especially good paper home from his CHAT (Calgarians Helping Aphasics Talk) group session. Normally right handed, he has learned to print amazingly well with his left hand—if he has words he can copy.

I looked at his handiwork in amazement. "Dennis, this is really great," I told him, "I used to put Tim and Rachel's papers up on the refrigerator when they did good work. You did so well on your paper, I'm putting it on the refrigerator."

We celebrate each new thing he can do, and turn ordinary days into celebrations by going out for lunch or stopping at McDonald's for an ice cream cone. Even a trip to the grocery store is an outing.

The doctor turned out to be right about Dennis being quite handicapped, especially in the area of speech. Do I ever feel disappointed that Dennis hasn't regained more speech? Yes, sometimes I do, but I don't dwell on it. Can I understand why God has given us this difficult journey? No. This is one of those mysteries we won't understand this side of heaven. But this doesn't shake my faith. I still believe in the goodness of God.

Recently Dennis wanted me to take him to a store in a shopping mall. I dropped him off, parked the car and then went into the pharmacy to see if he needed help. He was standing in front of the birthday section of a card rack, and waved me off, wanting to make his selection on his own. A while later, he came out with a smile on his face and a small bag in his hand.

The next week he presented me with a birthday card on my birthday. He had written Dennis Seever on the envelope as well as inside the card. The card was a beautiful tri-fold card with flowers on each panel. I read the verse that began with, "Every day is a gift from God." How had he chosen something that was so appropriate for me when he can't read? Tears came to my eyes.

Yes, life continues to be a challenge on a daily basis for both of us, but we hold on to hope. We travel this journey of ours one day at a time.

Calgary 2007. I cared for Dennis at home for 2³/⁴ years while working part-time. He went into a personal care home in March 2009.

Above left: The picture of the Persevering Trees (Story page 103).
Above right: Renylor (Tim's wife), Rachel, Janet, 2015.

Upper left: Dorothy Ausmus (Janet's mom) "Just One More Letter"
Upper Right: Rachel Seever. Lower Left: Shirley Seever (Dennis' mom)
Lower Right: Janet, taken in 1972 when she was teaching in Winsted, Minnesota

Above: Dennis, Tim and Andrew (Tim's son) taken 2009.

Left: Dennis and Janet at a family outing at Iron Horse Park in Airdrie, Alberta, riding on a small steam train. Summer 2019.

1986 – Janet, Tim, Dennis and Rachel. This was taken just before we left the U.S. for our assignment in Australia.

Experiencing God's Faithfulness

Life is full of surprises. If we could see into the future, we would draw back and say, "Lord, I don't think I can go through that." But it isn't our strength we rely on. The Lord is the One who supplies the strength we need in every situation.

When Dennis and I joined Wycliffe in 1975, we were committed to serving the Lord. Now with the passage of 36 ½ years, I am still as committed as I was then in seeing that minority groups get the Scriptures in their own languages. Back in 1975, 100 New Testaments had been published through Wycliffe's work, and now that number has reached more than 800, including some entire Bibles. But there is still more to do, with more than 2,000 languages still needing translation.

Over the years, Dennis and I served in a variety of places—Papua New Guinea; the Philippines; Darwin, Australia; and Dallas, Texas. In 1993, we moved to Canada to work at the Wycliffe Canada headquarters in Calgary, Alberta.

Then on a sunny Saturday—November 13, 2004—our lives were forever changed. On that day, Dennis had a major stroke, resulting in a life journey that has been frustrating, and sometimes overwhelming.

From the beginning, I chose not to see Dennis' stroke as a tragedy, but as a challenge, something we could work through with the Lord's help. My theme song has been Matt Redman's song, "Blessed Be the Name of the Lord." Yes, I've been "found in the desert place;" I've "walked through the wilderness;" and there has been "pain in the offering;" but I still can say, "blessed be Your name."

Now, after seven years, Dennis is still unable to talk, but I'm thankful he understands what we tell him. He can communicate by gestures, drawing pictures, or a simple yes or no. He walks with a cane, can't use his right hand, can't read or write and has extremely poor hearing (an inherited problem which compounds his other deficits). He has lost so many of the skills he used to have as a maintenance person and a bookkeeper in the Wycliffe finance office. Although he no longer lives at home during the week, I am deeply grateful that the personal care home where he has been living for the past three years provides safety, friendship with other people who have suffered brain injuries, birthday parties, barbecues in the summer, and an occasional mall excursion.

I'm also thankful that Dennis is able to come home for part of each weekend. He is still very much part of our family, and joins in family meals, birthday celebrations, trips and other activities. He is getting to know his four-year-old grandson, Andrew, who told me one time, "Grandpa is my best friend." How special is that? Andrew was born on November 13, 2007, three years to the *very day*, after his grandpa's stroke.

Dennis especially enjoys watching football on TV and riding his mobility scooter around the neighborhood to collect cans and bottles for recycling. His sense of direction is excellent.

While Dennis is at Waverley House during the week, I work at the Wycliffe office, where I edit a 20-page quarterly magazine, "Prayer Alive", which goes to 2,000+ Canadians and churches. In the magazine, we feature prayer requests of Canadian members. I also gather information on New Testament and Bible dedications and write a yearly article on dedications with Canadian involvement. Some of my time is spent writing an occasional press release, proofreading a wide variety of publications for the communications department, and assisting members with their newsletters.

The Lord has been with us throughout this difficult journey; we have reached a new "normal," with day-to-day living going more smoothly. Yes, I can truly say, "Blessed be Your name."

Calgary 2008. This was printed in a church newsletter in Minneapolis in 2008.

Just One More Letter

During the night of an ice storm in March 1957, my youngest sister was born. While Mom was in the hospital, my four-year-old sister and I, a 10-year-old, stayed with our paternal grandparents on the farm. My nine-year-old brother stayed with our maternal grandparents.

When the time came for Mom to bring baby Sharon home from the hospital, we were excited about going home as well. However, my sister and I started developing red spots—measles! The only way we were allowed to see our baby sister for the next two weeks was by walking on the hard-packed winter trail across a cornfield, going to the back of our house, and peering through the bedroom window.

Mom would tear an 8 ½ x 11 sheet of paper into quarters, and write a personal note to each of us every day. She would slide the bedroom window open far enough to pass the notes out to us. I delivered my brother's note to him on the school bus the next morning and carried my notes in my pocket. Those quarter-page notes were the first of many letters to come in the following years.

After graduating from high school in 1964, I moved from a small town of 2,000 to Minneapolis, 70 miles away. As a country girl, I found the city overwhelming—there were no wide-open spaces and the houses were too close together for my liking. I missed my family and the lake near our home. The University of Minnesota, which I attended that fall, had 40,000 students. It was many times larger than our entire town.

Mom's weekly letters, my source of encouragement, would arrive like clockwork. I wrote my letter on Sunday, she received it on Tuesday, and her reply would be in my mailbox on Thursday. Often when I had a tough day in class, Mom's letter would be waiting for me.

She wrote of ordinary things—what my dad was doing on the farm; who had gotten married, joined the army or had a baby; what my brother and sisters were doing; which elderly person at church had died; how her large garden was doing. Often the letters were written late at night, while she was finishing a batch of beans in the pressure cooker or had a kettle of tomatoes boiling on the stove. On more than one occasion, a spatter of tomato juice landed on the letter. "It's midnight now," she would write, "so I guess I should head to bed. I'm falling asleep while writing this."

After university, I worked at various jobs—in a medical research lab, as a teacher, and at a community college. One constant throughout that time was my mother's caring correspondence.

After I got married, my husband and I went overseas to do mission work in Papua New Guinea. I was so lonely at first that I would dream of being back home, only to wake up and find myself half a world away from all that was familiar. In 1977, personal computers didn't exist and we had no telephone, so letters were the only means of communication for the next four years. Mom's letters were my lifeline, my connection with home. By this time, my brother and two sisters were also away from home, so she was burning the midnight oil, as she would put it, writing to my siblings as well.

She now numbered the front of each envelope to make certain each one arrived safely, and surprisingly enough, they all did. It took two weeks for the letter to reach us, and two more weeks for my reply to get back to her. This was particularly worrisome when she had exploratory surgery for colon cancer. By the time the letter telling us that she would have surgery reached us, she had already had the surgery (her "grand opening", she called it), and it took another two weeks for us to learn the outcome! It turned out to be polyps, not cancer.

Our mission work eventually took us to the Philippines, Australia, and Dallas, Texas. In the late '80s, I began saving Mom's letters, knowing that someday she wouldn't be with us. I had no idea how soon that time would come.

My dad passed away in 1989 and we moved back to the

U.S. in 1990. After 26 years of weekly letters, Mom and I switched to talking on the telephone more often than writing.

Then in the spring of 1992, Mom came down with a mysterious illness. After many trips to doctors and courses of antibiotics, she only got worse. The whole family was with her in intensive care on a June evening as Jesus called her Home. I was holding her hand as she slipped away. She was 67.

There would be no more encouraging letters or phone calls. Later I found nearly 200 letters from her that I had saved. Sometimes I found a letter tucked away in a dresser drawer or as a marker in a recipe book. Nine years later, while cleaning out a storage shed, I even located some of those original quarter-page well-creased notes from 1957.

If I could write just one more letter to Mom, this is what I would say:

Mom, thanks for the unconditional love you showered on my siblings and me. You treated us all equally and had no favorites. Thanks for making do with so little when we were growing up. We never realized how poor we were materially, because we were rich in so many other ways. Thanks for your example of courage, faithfulness and determination as you lived out your life in situations that were often difficult. Thanks for making the time to write letters when you were too tired and too busy. You'll never know how much they encouraged me. Thank you for always providing a listening ear to your family and to many others. I thank God for the privilege of having you as my mother. Your grateful daughter, Janet

Calgary 2006. This appeared in several inspirational weekly e-mails sent to subscribers and I received responses from all over the world. One young woman in Africa was reconciled with her mother after reading it. My mother died in June 1992.

Thanks, Dad, Thanks

My father grew up as an only child of second-generation German immigrants, a rigid upbringing. In his early 20s, he married his high school sweetheart from a neighboring farm. I was the first of five children.

Dad expected his children to excel at school and whatever else they did. As the oldest, I worked hard to meet his expectations. In this era, fathers did not hug or kiss their children. Praise was sparse because it might "go to their heads and make them proud."

I remember a few occasions when we did things together. Dad carefully marked rows in the garden early each spring when the ground was still cold and damp. My brother and I followed him as he planted the first long rows of peas. I also remember planting spruce seedlings with him as part of a conservation project.

A few times I fished with Dad and my younger brother in Dad's old wooden boat. When the lake was high, huge sunfish hid around the roots of up-ended willow trees.

How I longed for Dad to say, "I love you" and give me a hug, but it never happened. Did he approve of me? It was difficult to tell in my teenage years.

I grew up, graduated from university, and eventually married. Unfortunately, my husband and I often lived hundreds of miles away from my family, and at times our work took us overseas. Mom wrote weekly, telling of events back home, what my dad was doing, and news of my siblings. But Dad never wrote. He left that up to Mom.

When we came home to the farm, our visits were cordial, but Dad and I were never close like some fathers and daughters.

In 1986, it was time to say goodbye for another of our overseas assignments. My husband, two children and I stood with Mom and Dad, our arms around each other. My husband prayed for God to watch over all of us while we were apart.

Afterward, I hugged Dad and said, "I love you." It was

still awkward.

"I love you too," he said and I noticed him brushing a tear from his eye. How I wished we had been closer over the years.

My parents were in their early 60s, so I expected to have many more times together in the future. We'd be back from our work in Australia in four years.

Then two-and-a-half years later, a life-shattering call came from home. That Sunday afternoon, Dad had been snowmobiling around the edge of the farm property, visiting neighbors. When he failed to return home, my brother-in-law searched for him and found him in the snow, dead of a massive heart attack.

Friends urged me to go home to Minnesota for the funeral. "You're not doing this for your father," they said. "You're doing this for yourself." How true it proved to be.

At the funeral, people had wonderful stories of Dad, a man of integrity with a quiet faith. Their stories were fresh; recent. They knew him so well. Even my youngest brother, 20 years younger than I, had related to Dad in a different way from me—as a friend.

Dad, how I wish I had really known you! I screamed inwardly. It was like a song without an ending, a book with the last pages torn out.

I grieved, for Dad and the close relationship that would never be.

Then, three years after his death, my mother died as well.

After the funeral, all of us five adult children came back to the farm and sifted through the treasures we had left behind in the attic of the family farmhouse. I was going through a box of my memorabilia when I came across a small canvas bag. Inside the bag were drawings I had done, old letters, and photos. In the midst, I discovered two letters from my dad, written years back when I was finishing university—the only personal thing I had in his handwriting. How could I have forgotten that they existed?

I carefully pulled out the yellowing paper. The first one was about things on the farm. The second was about an honor society I had been elected to at the university.

When I read the first paragraph of the second letter, my eyes welled with tears, for he had written, "How proud I am to have a daughter like you. . ."

Thanks, Dad. Thanks.

1992. Minnesota. My father died in February 1989.

Displaying Godly Contentment

The address on the envelope of the Christmas letter was one our friend Elaine had never used before. Had she moved, I wondered as I opened the envelope. I opened the letter and read. She quickly explained the reason for her change of address in her letter. After 30 years of teaching, and living in a major city, she had retired. She was now helping her 86-year-old dad take care of her 64-year-old brother who needed 24-hour supervision.

As I read those words, sadness swept over me. What a difficult situation Elaine must be in. I had no idea what the brother's problem was, but 24-hour care must certainly be burdensome to the caregivers.

However, as I continued to read, the next section reflected Elaine's feeling about the situation.

"There's hardly a dull moment, and we do have our ups and downs," she wrote. "Sometimes I feel a little bit like I am in the 'Little House in the Big Woods.' We are three-tenths of a mile off a gravel road that is off another gravel road. We overlook a pond. When we are not enjoying God's beautiful creation, we are either enjoying our favorite hobbies, or taking care of Gordy, my favorite brother."

Then it dawned on me. *My favorite brother*, she called him. Caring for Gordy was not a burden to her, but a privilege. Elaine displayed a graciousness I knew nothing of.

Am I as gracious when asked to do something that seems burdensome, or am I glad to serve? God calls us to be content in whatever situation we are in.

Written in 2003, a year before Dennis had his stroke. I knew nothing about being a caregiver at the time, but I soon found out.

No One Will Ever Know

Karen, Judy and I were the last ones back in the school room after lunch. We put our metal lunch boxes on the shelf above the coat hooks, which were mostly empty. All of the other sixth graders were already outside, playing marbles or hopscotch or jumping rope, since it was a pleasant spring day.

"Look what I found this morning in the storage cupboard when I was getting out some art supplies for Mrs. Eiffler." With a conspiratorial grin on her face, Karen held up a wooden box filled with short pieces of chalk in every color of the rainbow.

"Wow! What fun it would be to write on the chalkboard while everyone is outside." Judy's eyes twinkled with anticipation.

"But Mrs. Eiffler doesn't want us writing on the chalkboard," I responded, already feeling guilty, although we had not yet done a thing.

"Don't be such a 'fraidy cat', Janet. No one will ever know," said Karen, reaching into the box and drawing out a piece of chalk.

"Right. Everyone is outside, so we're safe. No one will tell on us." Judy was already drawing a house with sure strokes.

I reluctantly joined my friends in the artwork, wanting to be part of what was going on, but afraid of being caught. I knew well that we were breaking not one, but two class rules. The second rule was that no one was allowed to stay inside at noon without a written excuse from home if the weather was nice.

Trying various colors, we drew houses, trees and three-dimensional boxes. It was fun! All the time we were watching the clock, knowing that our fun would be over if anyone walked into the room.

Then Judy had an idea. "We're all right-handed. Let's see who can write their name best using their left hand."

Judy and Karen picked up their chalk and started writing. I chose a white piece from the box and wrote my name. The handwriting was a bit shaky, but no one would doubt that it said "Janet."

"I think Judy is the winner," said Karen. "Hers is the best."

"We'd better get this board cleaned off before Mrs. Eiffler comes back," said Judy, eying the clock. She picked up an eraser and began erasing our handiwork from the board.

Everything came off . . . but my name!

In disbelief, I looked at the chalk I held in my sweaty hand. On closer examination, it wasn't chalk at all. I had picked up a small piece of white color crayon that was mixed in with the pieces of chalk.

My stomach churned and my knees felt weak. What would Mrs. Eiffler do to me?

My mother had a saying: "Fools names and fools faces always appear in public places." I never understood fully what it meant before. Now I did! I was a fool, and there was my name in crayon to prove it. And the teacher would be returning soon.

"Quick, let's get some wet paper towels," said Judy, springing into action.

After vigorous rubbing, my name still remained.

"I think I saw a can of cleanser by the sink in the coat room," I said as I raced to find it. Precious minutes were ticking away.

We rubbed and my name came off all right, but in the process of removing it, we left an abrasion on the chalkboard.

Listening for footsteps coming down the hall, we dried the scrubbed area as much as we could with more paper towels and fanned it with a book to remove every tell-tale trace of wetness.

We were just slipping into our desks as the bell rang and the other students began entering the room. The teacher walked in soon afterward.

Mrs. Eiffler never asked about abrasion and maybe

never noticed it. But I did. Every time I walked past the marred surface of the chalkboard, I remembered. Oh, how I remembered.

The lesson I learned that day is one I never forgot, even though over 40 years have passed since the event. "No one will ever know" is never true. Even if no one else found out, God knew and I knew. Sometimes living with a guilty conscience is punishment enough.

1958. Pine City, Minnesota. This story of mine was found on a website by a Japanese company in 2014 and used in a workbook for Japanese students preparing for the English comprehension part of their university entrance exam. I was paid well for it and it was used twice.

Searching for Questions

A friend at work brought Tim to see me and introduced us. I looked up at the tall, handsome man standing before me.

"I remember you," he said, reaching down to give me a hug. I was mystified. As we talked, I found that I had known his parents while my husband and I were stationed on a missionary center overseas in the late 1970s. Tim, now 41, was in his teens at the time, and since my husband and I were newlyweds in our early 30s, we didn't really have any contact with the high school crowd. But for some reason, Tim still remembered us.

As we talked, I found that Tim and I had many mutual friends from that time—people he had known because they were friends of his parents, or parents of high school classmates.

He told me he was traveling through Canada and had stopped in Calgary on the way to see people who had worked in the mission at that time. He was reconnecting with his past.

"What kind of work are you doing now?" I asked, curious by this time.

"Nothing at the moment," he said. Then he explained that he had a university degree, but by the time he completed it, his field of training was obsolete because of rapidly advancing computer technology. To support himself, he had been working at a job that was below his level of education.

As he continued, I sensed he had a need to talk. An urgent need. I was more than willing to provide a listening ear, since it wasn't a busy morning for me.

A U.S. citizen and army officer, he told me he had just returned from a one-year tour of duty in Iraq six weeks earlier. That explained his present lack of a job.

"Wasn't it dangerous where you were?" I shuddered to think of what he had gone through.

"Not really," he responded. After reflecting a moment, he added, "One time I was hanging out my wash on a line, and the enemy blew holes through the 'Porta-Potty' near where I was standing."

And he didn't call that dangerous? Yikes!

Two weeks after he returned to the U.S., his wife died from complications of cancer and several strokes. From what he said, the marriage didn't sound like a happy one, but the change was traumatic nevertheless.

"It sounds like it's time to start over," I said.

He said he would like to, but first he had some of his wife's debts to clear up. He also wanted to get a master's degree through financing from his time in the service. Now he was traveling around the country and had stops planned for Canada, California, Texas, Florida, and finally back to his home area in Illinois. When he mentioned whom he would be visiting, they were people I knew as well.

"They're some quality people," I said, noting that they were former teachers from the school he had attended overseas.

"People are known by the company they keep," was his response.

When it was time for him to go, he gave me another hug. It had been a meaningful conversation for both of us. I was glad he had stopped because I, too, had a need to connect with the past. And I hoped my listening ear had been an encouragement to him.

The next thing he said greatly intrigued me. "I'm not searching for answers," he told me. "I'm searching for questions."

I'm searching for questions. I pondered that statement many times in the following days. What kind of questions would a 41-year-old man be looking for?

I could guess at some of them: What am I going to do with the rest of my life since it's probably half over? Is my life making a difference? If I died today, what would people remember about me? Have I touched anyone else's life? Is the world a better place because I have lived?

At least those are questions I've asked myself over the years.

So Tim, wherever you are, I hope you do find the questions you are searching for. And as you continue your path of life, may you find the answers as well. Life is too short and precious to waste any of it. God bless you on your journey.

2004 Calgary

Scattering Seeds to the Wind

When I was a young child, dandelions fascinated me. I would carefully pick a white globe of ripened seeds—I think we called them "lanterns"—making certain it was perfect. Then I would hold it up and blow, watching the seeds with their filmy parachutes drift along on the wind. I'm sure all of you have done what I'm describing. Who hasn't?

Inspirational stories on the Internet are like that. By sharing my inspirational stories, I'm scattering gospel seeds to the wind. Stories go much farther electronically than anything in print, sometimes even to countries where God's Word isn't welcome.

Meeting Readers Where They Are

From what I have seen this past year, people who read inspirational newsletters aren't necessarily the ones who buy Christian magazines or books, or read Sunday school papers and devotional booklets. They might not attend church or be Christians, but they're looking for something to jumpstart their day and warm their hearts like that first cup of morning coffee warms their bodies.

The names of inspirational newsletters and websites are indicative of this heart tug—HeartTouchers, heartwarmers, and 2theheart. Some sites are Christian; others are just positive and uplifting for readers of various religious persuasions. When so much of today's news is negative, the world needs something with a positive spin. Stories are short (700 words), uplifting and have less Scriptural teaching than devotionals.

Inspirational stories are also like dandelion seeds in that they tend to float from website to website (or newsletter to newsletter). Often editors of small inspirational websites or newsletters will contact the author and ask permission to reprint the article. Other times, because of people's ability to cut and paste, writing ends up in a wide variety of places beyond the author's control.

I was amazed to discover one of my stories was read on a country music radio station "Spirit of America" in Indianapolis, Indiana, and was posted on the station's website. Evidently someone liked it and submitted it. At least it still had my by-line and wasn't credited to "Author Unknown."

Some inspirational newsletter editors encourage readers to pass the newsletter along to friends as long as it is left intact with contact information and the by-lines.

Why Give Your Stories Away?

I've been asked, "Why do you give your stories away when you could sell them?" Good question. I no longer remember who asked me, but I've thought of it many times over this past year as I've explored the world of inspirational stories on the web.

Just why do I write for inspirational e-mail newsletters that "pay" only with a by-line? Again I go back to the fact that I'm scattering "gospel seeds." I consider it a ministry.

You might think that non-paying markets would attract only second-rate writers, but I assure you, that's not true—especially with the larger newsletters. Some of the writers have nationally syndicated columns or write regularly for their local newspapers. Others have been published numerous times in *Chicken Soup for the Soul, God Allows U-Turns*, and *Chocolate for a Woman's Heart*. A few have written books. One prolific writer makes his living as a motivational speaker and has his own newsletter. Writers often use their biographical sketch at the end of the article to advertise their own books or websites.

A large inspirational website states: "We can't pay you anything for your story, but we can make you famous! Many of our writers have gone on to sign book and magazine contracts. We have many publishers who subscribe to our service and they are always looking for new talent . . ."

Making a Difference

The biggest reward of writing inspirational articles for the Internet is getting reader feedback. Since my e-mail address is included in my biographical sketch, response comes readily from people who wouldn't normally respond to a newspaper or magazine article. I've gotten e-mails from Switzerland, the Philippines, Zimbabwe, Colombia, Nigeria, South Africa and the United Arab Emirates, as well as the U.S. and Canada. And those are only the readers who have identified where they live.

One reader read my story about praying for an impossible co-worker and wrote, "Just before I read the story, I had been praying silently on how to interact with a person much like in the story. God's timing is impeccable, as the story helped answer my prayer."

In response to an "angel" story of mine, a reader wrote in the subject line, "Please write back." Then she asked me to pray for her husband who was undergoing tests. I responded that I would, and a week later decided to check with her. Her husband's cancer test had turned out negative. At that point I learned Debbie and her husband are Christians from India who have lived in the United Arab Emirates (UAE) for 10 years. Christians there are a persecuted minority and Christian books and videos sent through the mail are confiscated. "We have had no Christian fellowship for 10 years," she wrote, and said she very much would like a Christian friend. Could I find one for her?

When I mentioned Debbie to friends in my Bible study, one person knew of a couple who had done short term mission work in UAE. Through a series of contacts, I found a friend for Debbie who lives in her city. Debbie and her family were able to visit Vera and her family and they attended church together! Debbie is delighted—and so am I. Although she has some major struggles, I am amazed at what the Lord is doing in this woman's life week by week. We've been exchanging password-protected e-mails for two months.

Another reader read the same "angel" story and wrote, "I found your story inspirational. I'm searching for God and I hope to find Him soon."

I wrote back, "If you are searching for God, then you have made a good first step. He is searching for you even more than you are searching for Him." Then I explained the Steps to Peace with God (Billy Graham Association). In the next e-mail, Melanie said she had gone through the steps I shared with her. She then told me she had been a committed Christian 10 years ago, but through a series of difficulties had become bitter and angry, and turned away from God.

I've had the joy of encouraging her as she has been taking steps toward the Lord. It's exciting to know I can reach across the world electronically—Melanie lives in South Africa.

"God is moving in my life in a remarkable way, but I am not surprised," she wrote recently. "I made a recommitment to Him this weekend and His peace envelops me. I am much calmer now."

My Bible study group prays for both Melanie and Debbie, who both readily share their prayer requests.

Did I say I don't get paid? That's not quite the truth. Who can put a value on a person coming back to the Lord? Or a person finding Christian fellowship after searching for 10 years? I'd say I've been paid very well. The scattered seeds are beginning to grow.

2006 Calgary. Published in FellowScript *magazine, a publication of InScribe Christian Writers' Fellowship of Canada. In 2008, a pastor in India read the angel story that I had written online and began corresponding with me. I now help support the 50 orphans in Joy's Orphans Home and they call me "grandma."*

This is My House

February 4, 2006, was a night like no other. I hadn't slept well for some reason, and at 3:30 a.m., just as I was drifting back to sleep, the light in our bedroom went on. A man was standing by our bed, glaring down at my husband and me! He had a short haircut and a goatee like our son Tim, who lives in our basement apartment, but when I got my eyes to focus, it definitely was not Tim. Barrel chested, the young man wore a black sweatshirt and two gold earrings.

"You're sleeping in my bed!" Anger rose in his voice. "You're living in my house! I've got papers to prove it."

It was no dream. This was real. "Who are you?" I asked, "What's your name?" to which he responded, "Ron."

I needed a phone, but it was in the kitchen. My husband woke up momentarily, but since he is handicapped from a stroke, he could do nothing to help. I had no way to contact my son in the basement. So it was just Ron and I as the drama unfolded.

"Let's go to the kitchen and talk about this," I said, getting out of bed and heading for the hall. I could tell Ron had been drinking because I could smell alcohol, although his speech wasn't slurred. Strangely enough, I was perfectly calm.

Still angry, Ron followed me to the kitchen. "So this is your house?" I asked.

"Yes, I paid for it. But I suppose you need your sleep," he responded.

"If it's your house, would the police kick us out?" He agreed they would. "Shall I call them and see?" This was the opportunity I was looking for.

"It's 911," said Ron. He quit his tirade about owning the house and relaxed. When I asked him how he had gotten here, he said that the cab had dropped him off at the front door of "his house" and he had just walked in. Then I remembered—my husband had let in the cat before we went to bed, and I hadn't checked to see if he had relocked the door.

So I called 911. I calmly explained to the woman at the other end that I had a man in my kitchen, who said he owned the house we were living in. She transferred me to the police department.

During our conversation, the police dispatcher said, "You sound calm," to which I agreed. "Is he threatening you?"

"You aren't threatening me, are you, Ron?" He said "No."

I told the woman on the phone that he only wanted his house back. (I hoped she didn't think I was too calm and dismiss this as a prank call.)

Ron was completely cooperative, answering questions about himself for the police dispatcher on the other end of the line as I relayed the questions to him—he was 5'10", 300 pounds (I think he was mistaken about that), 27 years old, dressed in a black shirt and sweatshirt.

"I've got pants on too."

He then rolled up his sleeve to show me he had a tattoo. He also gave us his full name this time.

Shortly afterward, we heard the door open—It was still unlocked. Two police officers entered. "Do you still think you own this house?" they asked Ron as he walked toward the door. At this point he had sobered up enough to agree that the house didn't look anything like his, and he gave them his address in the next subdivision.

"I've never seen this woman before in my life," he said, referring to me. He apologized profusely for entering our house by mistake.

But I said it was just Ron and me. That's not really true. I think God had His angels encamped around me. And getting Ron to agree to my phoning the police? I don't normally think that clearly in the middle of the night, especially in stressful situations. I think God gave me the words to say.

2006 Calgary. This appeared in a book by InScribe Christian Writers' Fellowship called InScribed – 30 Years of Inspiring Writers. *2010.*

The Lord Hasn't Forgotten Me

Solitude. A time of reflection and prayer. That's why I drove two-and-a-half hours from Calgary to a small retreat center in a wooded area, built by friends of mine. They added two extra bedrooms in their walk-out basement and a little apartment above their garage for missionaries and Christian workers who need a time of reflection and prayer—or just to get away from the hustle and bustle of the city. That's what I need right now!

Sitting on a porch swing in back of their house, I hear wind chimes and leaves rustling as the wind plays tag with the aspen trees. The Clearwater River—sparkling in the sun— rushes below the steep embankment, peeking between the young trees that line the bank.

I have books with me as well as my Bible: *Prayer—Does It Make a Difference?* by Philip Yancey, *Living Light* (a devotional book) and some other publications. My prayer is that the Lord will make the path ahead clear to me.

As I open my book to read, I hear the familiar sound of chick-a-dees, little birds I remember well from my childhood days, calling out their name *chick-a-dee-dee-dee* as they fly past me. These sounds I hear, but do I hear God's voice in the midst of other distractions? That's important; it's the reason I am spending time here alone.

On this August day, I have more questions than answers. I'm 64, but still have no definite retirement plans for the time in the future when I am no longer capable of working.

My husband is severely disabled from a very large stroke six years ago that left him unable to read, write or speak. It also affected his reasoning ability and the use of his right hand; he walks slowly with a cane. He now lives in a personal care home, which takes much of the pension he is receiving. We had planned to be together when retirement came, but those plans are no longer working.

I've already done the calculations, and don't see how I'll have enough funds when the time comes. Now I'm wondering—just what happens next? All of this weighs heavily on my mind. How I need God's wisdom in the midst of all of this! As missionaries in a faith mission, we have seen God provide for our family in so many ways in the past. So why am I now having difficulty trusting Him for the future? Good question.

While I'm reading *Living Light*, I come across the verses from Isaiah 49:15b, 16a (NIV): " . . . I will not forget you. Behold, I have graven you on the palms of my hands." I think about it along with some other meaningful verses and copy them into my notebook. How meaningful those verses in Isaiah are! God won't forget me! I think about it for a while.

Then as I go for a walk down the gravel road to get some exercise, I notice the wild rose bushes, milkweed plants with pods and clover along the way. During my walk I find five four-leaf clovers. People think that four-leaf clovers are lucky, but I see them as a novelty and have often found them in the past. I don't believe in luck; my trust is in God. However, right now "trusting an unknown future to a known God" is in my head, but not yet in my heart.

Back from my walk, I settle down with Philip Yancey's book, *Prayer—Does It Make a Difference*? A friendly cat named Tika settles next to me, purring as she enjoys the August sunshine. Reaching over, I pet her absent-mindedly. Suddenly I am startled as I read, for I have encountered the *same* verses from Isaiah 49: ". . . I will not forget you. Behold I have graven you on the palms of my hands." Wow! It's not a frequently quoted verse so I don't normally encounter it on a regular basis, certainly not twice in one day. Is God trying to tell me something?

Later that afternoon, my friend Barry—who owns the retreat center along with his wife—gives me a booklet he thinks I might like to read. I have told him nothing about my encounter with the Isaiah 49 verses, but there on the cover of that booklet are the *same verses*. Isaiah 49: 15b-16a. God has not forgotten me!

When I randomly turn to an article inside the booklet, the *entire* article is based on Isaiah 49:15b-16a: "I will not forget you. Behold, I have graven you on the palms of my hands."

In all, during those two days at the retreat center, I encounter those two verses *six* times! Can I explain it? No, not at all. It's a message God wanted me to understand. *Six times. Yes, Lord, I'm hearing you, loud and clear.* I've rarely felt God's love in such a dramatic, personal way.

So did I find answers to my questions? No. But the Lord let me know in the most amazing way that He hasn't forgotten me. And for now, that's more than enough.

2010. Rocky Mountain House, Alberta.

To See Him More Clearly

(devotional)

For we live by faith, not by sight (2 Corinthians 5:7 NIV).

After three years of various eye challenges—cataract surgery, a glaucoma diagnosis, a corneal ulcer, and a severe allergic reaction to glaucoma medication, my eyes had reached a point of stability. It was time to get a new prescription for glasses. I was having difficulty reading street signs, so I booked an appointment with Dr. Sanders, my optometrist.

Dr. Sanders concluded his eye exam. "Your current prescription is the correct one," he said, "except you now have more astigmatism in your right eye. However, your macular degeneration has progressed over the past year." (I've had the beginning of macular degeneration for seven years, but it was stable previously.)

A feeling of sadness swept through me. *My vision will never be better than it is right now*, I thought. *In fact, it will get progressively worse.* My mind raced ahead to thoughts of blindness, of no longer being able to drive, of no longer being able to read or see my computer screen. I went home and grieved my impending losses; I'm a writer and need my eyes. Friends had prayed for me during my previous eye challenges, so I shared my anguish with my Facebook friends.

A friend wrote, "One day, this day, is all we're called to live. May the Lord give you joy each and every day, and may His hand be upon your eyes." Yes, she was right. We can only live one day at a time. Then I read a quote by Dr. Tony Evans: "Worrying is assuming that God doesn't know what He is doing." That was true too. Worrying about the future wouldn't do me any good. God already knows what's happening in my future, and He walks there with me. I need to live by faith in His goodness and care.

But what really encouraged me were words from the

musical Godspell that another friend shared with me. "Day by day, dear Lord, I pray: To see you more clearly, Love you more dearly, Follow you more nearly, day by day." *Yes! I need to fix my eyes on Jesus and see Him more clearly,* I thought. I now have these words posted above my desk at work, and think about them each day.

Isn't that what we all want—to see God more clearly?

Prayer: Dear Lord, in times of distress, teach us to keep our eyes on You. Help us to see You more clearly, love You more dearly** and follow You more nearly. Amen.

** *Godspell. A condensed version of this was used in* The Upper Room *(a devotional booklet or online version that goes to 4 million people) in early 2019.*

Who Is My Neighbor?

I first rang her doorbell as a volunteer, collecting funds for the Cancer Society in April 2002. The weather was still chilly, but tulips had already poked through the ground and were beginning to open in front of her house.

The dark-haired woman from South Asia who answered the door told me she wasn't interested.

"But nearly everyone has a relative or friend dealing with cancer," I said. "I'm here as a volunteer because my grandmother died of cancer many years ago."

The expression on her face softened. "I had cancer surgery over 10 years ago," she said with a heavy accent. "Please come in."

She served me tea and told me her story. She and her family had been in Canada for only two years and she had very few friends. A lonely woman, she seemed eager to have someone to talk with. I wasn't at all sorry I wasn't able to finish my collection route that afternoon. After all, she was my neighbor, just five houses down from me.

"Please come back again and visit me," Shandah* said as I was leaving. So I did.

I learned about her family and her customs. She had grown up in a Muslim country as a Muslim but had attended a Catholic school as a child. She had heard the story of Jesus in school.

"When I was growing up, I wanted to be a nun," she said with a laugh.

I told her I was a Christian, which was fine with her. "All religions are good," she said.

I visited her every week or two so she had someone to practice English with, and because she was lonely. It was her custom to stay in her house. She wasn't used to doing housework and cooking because she had servants in her homeland to do those things. To fill in her spare time, she often did lovely oil paintings, which filled her walls.

Before coming to visit, I'd call her and ask, "Do you want

a visit today?" to which she would respond with a cheery, "Sure, why not?"

We'd greet each other with a hug and she would bring out orange juice, cake or some type of pastry, nuts, and tea. Gracious hospitality was her custom. Each visit ended with a large cup of tea with milk and sugar.

When her daughter was going through severe marriage problems, Shandah vented her frustration, and I provided a listening ear. My Bible study group prayed for her and her family, which was fine with her.

One time we watched the *JESUS* film together in her national language. Her response was that she had heard it before. "I wish Bush would watch this film," she said, anger rising in her voice. (It was the beginning of the Iraq war in 2003.) "Because President Bush should love his neighbor?" I ventured, not certain just what her response would be.

"Yes," she responded, fire in her eyes. I quickly let the subject drop and didn't have the heart to tell her that President Bush already knew the content of the film.

When she studied for her test to become a Canadian citizen, I spent several of my visits asking her questions from the handbook. She passed with flying colors.

One time in the summer of 2003 she was eager to tell me about a dream she had. (Dreams have great significance in her culture). Three people in the dream put a bracelet on her arm. On the bracelet was a picture of a man with a crown on his head like a king. "Who is that?" she asked, to which the people in her dream responded, "That's Jesus. He will protect you." That dream had significance to her, and it was one of our topics of conversation in the following weeks.

Soon after that, I gave her a paper with Bible verses and "Steps to Peace with God." "Just pray the prayer if you are in really dangerous circumstances or afraid you are dying," I told her.

Early in 2004, because of various family circumstances, she and her husband felt they should return to their homeland in South Asia. As they prepared, I visited her, knowing how I would miss her when she left. Then one day in February, she had trouble breathing. Her doctor did a bone scan and a lung scan and checked the fluid in one of her lungs for cancer cells. Was her cancer back after nearly 15 years?

Wanting some way to encourage her, I went to a Christian bookstore and searched for a bracelet like the one in her dream, but none like it existed. However, I got a bracelet with the words 'faith,' 'peace,' 'friend,' 'courage,' and 'love' on it. I also bought a Bible Promise book and marked the pages with verses on "fear" and "God's protection." When I showed her the topic, "God's Protection," Shandah's eyes widened with surprise. So what she had seen in her dream really was in the Bible!

I helped her with her packing as she and her husband moved out of their house. Awaiting results of her cancer test, they stayed with another family. Then suddenly, without any warning or saying goodbye, they left for South Asia. I wrote several times, but when I heard nothing from her, I called her overseas phone number. Sadness filled her voice as she answered the phone. "I'm not good," she said. "I just couldn't write to you and tell you." Cancer was back in one of her lungs and she was now on chemo. Her doctor in Canada had told her she absolutely could not fly, but she and her husband had flown back anyway. I had guessed as much. The struggle she faces with her illness will be hard. I assured her of my prayers and prayed for her over the phone.

Today as I walked down the block, I noticed the tulips in front of her old house are once again up and will soon be turning the garden into a rainbow of colors. What a vivid reminder they are of my special friend, Shandah.

As I look around my own house I see reminders of my friend everywhere as well. Before leaving, she gave me four of her large plants, her beautiful coffee table and end table set (because I had once made a joke about not having a coffee table), and a variety of other smaller items—all from the heart. I am sad, but my life is richer because of knowing her.

Someone once asked Jesus, "Who is my neighbor?" Jesus followed with the story of the Good Samaritan. In my case, my "neighbor" was a lonely stranger far from her home culture who needed God's love. And through that shared love, she became a special friend.

Name changed and homeland called "South Asia" because she comes from a Muslim country where Christians are a persecuted minority. 2004 Calgary. My friend died within a couple years of going back to her home country.

Perseverance

When I think of perseverance, it reminds me of the two stately spruce trees in our back yard. In 1995, Dennis discovered spruce seedlings in the flower bed in front of our house. They were about an inch tall. The next year I planted seven of them in a planter. When they were big enough, I planted them in a row behind our house. Now, years later, two of them remain. It's a reminder just to keep going in life's storms. The trees are now over 20-feet tall (see photo on page 70).

The Christmas Angel

"**I** like that ceramic angel in the corner best, Gram," said Amanda. "She's so pretty."

Her grandmother leaned over and peered into the glass case that held her angel collection—ceramic, glass and carved wood. When Amanda came for a visit, they often looked at the angels.

"Are angels real? Do they watch over us?" Amanda always had a million questions—and that's only a slight exaggeration. Gram loved her for her inquisitive mind.

"The Bible speaks of angels many times. There are Michael and Gabriel, and the book of Hebrews speaks of 'angels unaware' among us," Gram answered. "Of course there were angels at Jesus' birth. I've also heard that we have guardian angels, but I've never given it much thought."

"Do you know 'Angels Watching over Me'?" Amanda sang a line in the sweet, clear voice of a 13-year-old, and Gram joined in. "All day, all night, angels watching over me . . ."

After that they settled back on the heavy black leather couch in the living room and munched on popcorn they had popped in a frying pan on the wood-burning stove in the farm kitchen. They both had hot cocoa with marshmallows. Labour Day weekend was a special time Amanda spent with her grandmother each year.

"Please tell me the story about when you were teaching in the country school," Amanda begged, never tiring of it.

"I was just 19 at the time," Gram began. "I was teaching in a one-room school on the Prairies. One day I sent Edwin to the back of the room to sit in the corner because he was misbehaving. Instead, he crawled out the window. He was more man than boy at 17, but was only in eighth grade because his dad often kept him home to work on the farm."

"Then what happened, Gram?" asked Amanda, although she knew the story so well she could tell it herself.

"I called him back in and scolded him for being disobedient. He was so tall he towered over me. He just looked down

FICTION

at me and said, 'Little girl.' I blushed. After that we came to an understanding and I never had any more trouble with him."

"A couple years later he joined the army, and then I heard he was killed in the Great War in Europe—World War I," Gram said sadly, as if it had happened just yesterday instead of 40 years ago.

"How does God decide when people have lived long enough and it's time for them to die?" The thought of Edwin dying so young troubled Amanda.

"Oh, Amanda Jane, you're always so full of questions." Gram smiled. "I remember other questions you had when you were younger. 'How long is forever?' 'How far does the universe go?' 'Who would I be if I hadn't been born?' I didn't have good answers for those, and this is a tough one as well. Let me think about it."

She paused a moment, and then continued. "One thing I can tell you is that God knows everything about us and our times are in His hands. The Bible says that even the hairs on our heads are numbered. We don't need to be afraid."

"Gram, I hope you don't die for a long, long time. I couldn't stand it if you did."

"Only God knows the future," said Gram, changing the subject. "Have you finished reading that book by Lucy Maude Montgomery? I think you would be a kindred spirit with Anne of Green Gables."

"Oh, Gram, I hope I can visit Prince Edward Island when I grow up. That would be extraordinarily special."

The next day Amanda hugged Gram goodbye while her mother waited for her near the door. Their Manitoba farms were only three miles apart, so they saw each other often.

"I'm so looking forward to spending a week at Christmas with you just like last year. I want to string popcorn and cranberries for the Christmas tree." Amanda's words tumbled out. "Can I help pick the tree out in the woods with Grandpa? Maybe after that you can teach me to crochet—not doilies, but something useful."

"Whoa, slow down long enough to take a breath, dear girl." Gram laughed her musical laugh.

Fall came to the farm. Leaves turned brilliant colors, drifting to the ground one by one. Amanda's two younger brothers, Tom and Johnny, made huge piles and then jumped in them. At 13, she knew she was too old to play in leaves, so she did it when no one was watching.

At home Amanda helped her mother freeze and can vegetables from their garden. When she wasn't helping or working on homework, she was on a quest. She got her Bible down from the shelf and started reading it. Previously, she only used it to look up verses in Sunday school. She found the concordance and began looking up verses on death and angels.

In a notebook, she wrote down questions she needed to answer.

Are there angels around us? Can we recognize them?

How does God decide when it's time for people to die?

Can I find comfort in the Bible like Gram does in hers?

At Thanksgiving, everyone jumped into the car for a trip to see Gram and Grandpa. Mom made salads, vegetables and homemade rolls. Gram prepared the turkey, dressing, potatoes and pumpkin pie.

"Hi, Amanda, Tom and Johnny. It's so good to see you," Gram greeted them. "I hope you brought hearty appetites with you." The aroma of a Thanksgiving feast floated from the kitchen.

After watching Gram that day, Amanda could tell she wasn't feeling well. She didn't laugh like she normally did, and her face looked pained. She and Amanda didn't even get around to looking at the angel collection, a Thanksgiving tradition.

When they got home, Amanda confronted her mother. "Mom, Gram wasn't feeling well. I could tell. Do you know what's wrong?"

"She's been having some pain. The doctor will be doing some tests next week." Mom had a worried expression on

FICTION

her face, the same kind of expression she had the year the crops had failed. "Pray for your grandmother, Amanda."

"I will. I always do."

After checking Gram, the doctor sent her to a hospital in Winnipeg. Amanda's mother went to Winnipeg to stay with relatives who lived there so she could visit Gram. With the responsibility of making meals for her dad and brothers, Amanda was glad Mom had left prepared meals in the freezer and that the neighbors helped supply some food. The house was lonely without Mom. Amanda tried to focus on positive things and not worry about Gram, but Gram was continuously on her mind.

"Gram has cancer," said Mom when she phoned home several days later. "The doctors removed a large tumor, but it has spread throughout her body." Amanda had never encountered anyone with cancer before, but she knew cancer was deadly.

"God, please let Gram live," she earnestly prayed.

Amanda usually rode home from school on the school bus with Tom and Johnny. However, two weeks later, she knew something was wrong. Dad was waiting for them at the school and had an anguished expression on his face.

He said nothing, but waited until they all got into the car. "Gram died today. The doctors tried very hard, but they couldn't save her."

After the five-mile ride home, Amanda rushed into the house. Mom was back at home and Amanda could tell that she had been crying. She gave her mother a quick hug. Then she ran to her room, threw herself down on her bed and cried for hours.

They went through the motions of Christmas that year. It was a sad time and no one was really in the mood to celebrate. Amanda, of course, could not spend the week with Gram. Grandpa didn't even get a tree from the woods. On Christmas Day they opened the few presents they had. Finally, they were down to the last present.

"Amanda, this last one is yours." Tom handed her a package.

The handwriting on the outside was her mother's. But immediately when Amanda opened the package, she knew it was from Gram. It contained an exquisite crocheted angel about six inches high. Next to the angel was a note in her grandmother's handwriting.

Amanda Jane, here is "an angel to watch over you." I finished it just before I came to the hospital. I will be in surgery tomorrow, and I don't know what the future holds. But I know Who holds the future. Don't be afraid. I'm looking forward to being with Jesus if that is what He has for me. Here is a Bible verse for you from Hebrews 13:5: ". . .for he hath said, I will never leave thee, nor forsake thee." Remember that Jesus is with you forever. He will never abandon you.
Love forever, Gram

Amanda clutched the angel as tears streamed down her face. How could a Christmas be this sad and this special at the same time? She knew she would treasure Gram's last gift —the Christmas angel—and her example of faith forever.

This won first prize in the fiction division of InScribe Christian Writer's Fellowship contest in 2005.

FICTION

A Glimmer of Hope (Fiction)

Downy snowflakes fell on the bare tree branches; they fell on the charred wood scattered outside of the house at 319 Elm Street, covering the evidence of the fire the previous night; and they fell on Connie Barrett, melting on her face and mingling with her tears.

Connie looked up at the roof, or what was left of it. Huge plastic tarps covered the gaping hole where the fire had burned through. Living in the basement apartment, she and her boys had escaped through a bedroom window when smoke came billowing down the stairway.

As the afternoon daylight faded, Connie walked over to the window, knelt down and peered in to see what of her worldly possessions remained; it was difficult to see anything, but it appeared that the basement had suffered mostly smoke damage. However, the firemen had told her no one could enter the house. Structural damage to the stairs and some other places, they said. It made it too dangerous. She could go in after the damage was assessed and the cause of the fire determined. But it would probably be a month before she could move back in. Just guessing from past experience, they said.

Connie wiped her eyes with a tissue and stuffed it back into her pocket.

Never before had she felt so alone and helpless. She and her eight-year-old twins, Tony and Tyler, had moved to this place two months ago after Robert, her husband of 10 years, had packed up and moved out of their house. Just like that, he was gone and she was alone. She should have seen it coming. Robert had a restlessness she never understood — always moving and changing jobs. It was his idea to move from Ontario to Alberta six months ago. Now she was a stranger here; all of her friends and family lived out east.

"God, are You up there someplace? Do you care?" she asked, desperately wanting answers, but not really expecting any. She was being tossed about in the raging storms of life. Connie knew she needed something to cling to, but she had nothing. Absolutely nothing.

Across the street at 318 Elm, Hazel Wilcox sat by the window, rocking gently in her pink flowered rocking chair. She had been reading her Bible which now lay in her lap as she idly watched snowflakes fall. Sunny, her collie, nuzzled her hand and whined.

"Sorry, boy. You wouldn't like walking in all this snow. Besides, I already took you out for a walk earlier today—or maybe it was you who took me." At 62, she was finding that arthritis made walking increasingly more difficult.

"I know you miss Roger," she said as she scratched Sunny's head. "He always took you for a walk when he got home from work. This is going to be a sad Christmas because he's not here." A tear escaped her eye as she thought of her husband who had died of a heart attack six months earlier.

"Lord, do you have much left for this old woman to do? Because I don't feel very useful down here any more. I try hard not to feel sorry for myself, but I don't always succeed."

Then Hazel chuckled to herself. "Sorry, Lord. I'm just not myself today. When I whine, I probably sound like Sunny."

At that moment, movement across the street caught her eye. Connie! She would recognize that distinctive blue parka anywhere.

Last night Hazel had watched the firemen battling the flames and prayed for the people living there. What a relief it was to hear that Connie and her boys and the couple who lived upstairs had gotten out safely. Now Connie was standing there, looking at the house.

Hazel knew Connie from the times they talked when she was walking Sunny in front of Connie's apartment. Some days Hazel did more talking than walking.

Suddenly Hazel felt an urgent need to put on her coat and walk across the street.

FICTION

She was out of breath by the time she reached the forlorn figure staring at the house. "Connie, I'm so sorry about the fire."

Grief written all over her face, Connie turned and looked at her. "Thanks for your concern, Hazel. I didn't need this fire just when I was trying to get back on my feet."

"Where are you staying?" Hazel pulled her knitted cap more tightly on her head and shivered in the cold.

"I'm at the women's shelter." Connie dabbed her eyes again with the soggy tissue. "I didn't quite qualify as a battered wife since my husband is no longer at home, but they agreed I couldn't live on the street. The boys are at the shelter now. One of the ladies there said she would watch them."

"Were you able to get anything from the house?" asked Hazel.

"No, I can't go in yet." Connie sighed wearily. "I got some things from the Salvation Army so at least the boys can have clothes to wear. And I got a few things to wear for my job at the bank."

"Christmas is coming next week," Hazel said hesitantly. "I know you're from out of town. Would you like to have Christmas with us? My son and daughter and their families are coming over. You and your boys are more than welcome to join us."

"We weren't going to have much of a Christmas this year." Connie was thoughtful, on the verge of more tears. "Sharing Christmas with you would give me something to look forward to. Thank you so very much."

"I'll see you soon. God bless you," said Hazel, turning to go. By now the icicle lights were starting to twinkle on some of the houses along the block. Forgetting her arthritis, Hazel walked with a new spring in her step. She thought about Christmas and being able to encourage a family who didn't have the means to help themselves. She could actually do something! She forgot that she was feeling useless.

The next day she put a Christmas music tape in her tape deck and found herself singing Christmas carols as she wrapped small gifts for Connie and her boys. At one time she had been a soprano in the church choir and even sang solos. Now her voice again filled the room.

A few days later, Hazel actually had fun making apple pies—her specialty—ahead of time for the celebration. She would also do the turkey. Her daughter Karen would be bringing a few things and her daughter-in-law, Suzanne, had volunteered a few items as well.

Days passed swiftly and Christmas Day arrived. In a flurry of excitement, Hazel's children and her four grandchildren—now in their teens—stomped the snow off their boots as they entered the hallway. Christmas music filled the house, and the fragrance of pine, spicy apple cider and turkey wafted through the air. Laughter soon blended in with the clanging of pots and pans in the kitchen.

Then the doorbell rang. "I'm sorry we're a little late, Hazel," Connie apologized. "Bus connections are horrible on holidays, but I can't afford a car."

Her two sons bounded in with enthusiasm. Tyler found Sunny and put his arms around the dog's neck. "Sunny, you're a good dog." Sunny's tail thumped against the floor as he licked Tyler's face.

"This house smells just like my grandma's house at Christmas," said Tony wistfully. "I sure miss her."

"I'm sure you do," said Hazel as she helped them with their coats.

A short time later everyone was seated at the food-laden table. After Hazel arranged the turkey in the center, she turned to her son. "Sean, would you like to ask the blessing?"

When Sean finished, Tony piped up, "My grandpa always prays before meals too. Mom, why can't we do that at home?"

"Maybe some day we can," said Connie, letting the conversation drop there. She was deep in thought. It had been a long time since she had gone to church as a child. What did she believe? Was there hope for her? Did Christmas

FICTION

have more meaning than just a festive holiday?

After they finished their meal, Sean got out the family Bible from the bookcase and read the Christmas story — a family tradition.

Waves of nostalgia spread through Connie as she remembered hearing the Christmas story read at home as a child. Suddenly she felt homesick. So very homesick.

Later they all opened presents. "Oh, there are presents for us too!" squealed Tyler.

A broad grin spread across Tony's face. "Cool."

After the presents were opened, Hazel, Karen, Suzanne and Connie went to the kitchen to do dishes. Hazel turned to Connie. "What are you finding the most difficult now days?"

"I dread getting the boys to school on the city bus and then finding a connecting bus to get to my work on time. The shelter is so far from Clearbrook Elementary School."

Hazel thought for a minute. "I have a big family room and a bedroom downstairs. My house has been empty since my children grew up and left to get married. How would you like to move in with me until your house is fixed? It would save you the long bus trip."

"I have a microwave and a small refrigerator which we aren't using," offered Karen. "You're welcome to use them."

"No one has ever been so kind to me before." Connie's voice was choked with emotion. "Thank you so much."

After Hazel's children and grandchildren left in the late afternoon, the house grew quiet. Connie could hear her sons laughing as they watched one of the "Veggie Tales," videos Hazel had gotten when her grandchildren were young.

Noticing Hazel's Bible on the table by her rocking chair, Connie said shyly, "Would you mind if I ask you a personal question?"

"I don't mind."

"I see you have a Bible. Do you read it?" Connie was now looking intently at Hazel. "Do you believe it?"

"I don't think I would have survived the many ups and

downs of life without my faith in God," said Hazel fervently, "especially after Roger's death. Yes, I do believe the Bible."

"Well, I've been noticing something missing in my life lately. I haven't found anything to fill the emptiness," Connie continued sadly. "My parents believe in God. I gave up most of what I believed in college, and being married to Robert destroyed the rest."

Both were silent for a few minutes. Then Connie said, "I was wondering if the boys and I could come to church with you. I want to find what I lost."

"Honey, God has already been searching for you far more than you have been searching for Him. Of course you can come to church with me."

Connie looked at her watch. "We have just enough time to make it to the bus stop. I'll be back tomorrow night with my things."

She gave Hazel a warm hug. Hazel reached down and hugged Tony and Tyler who reminded her of when her own grandchildren were younger.

"I'll be praying for you," Hazel assured them. "Merry Christmas."

That night Hazel sat reflecting in her rocking chair. "Thank you, Lord. It was a much better Christmas than I imagined it would be. You let me help Connie at a time when I was feeling useless. Please help her find You."

On the other side of the city, Connie snuggled under the blankets in her bed at the women's shelter for one last night. Across the room, she could hear the quiet breathing of her sons who had fallen into an exhausted sleep, still clutching their Christmas toys from Hazel.

Hope had eluded Connie for so long in the past. Now she saw a glimmer of hope for the first time in months, maybe years. "God, thank you for sending Hazel just when I needed a friend," she whispered. "Now I believe in You."

"A Glimmer of Hope" was printed in the book, The Essence Collection: Celebrating the Season *in 2001.*

FICTION

A Journey Through Time

Glancing at her watch, Sandra knew she had exactly two hours. She grabbed a box of tissues and made herself a cup of tea. She got out the box of old journals, spreading the contents in front of her. The passages she wanted were already marked, but now there was an urgency to her journey through time.

Taking a sip of her tea, she picked up the journal marked 1973-1975 and began to read.

October 5, 1973. Today I encountered a rude man at the checkout counter—but I was equally rude to him. (God, please forgive me.) As I was approaching the "12 items only" check out line, a man in his 30s raced in front of me and plopped his basket on the counter. Turning to me, he said, "I hope you don't mind. I think I'm going to be late for an appointment." "Well, I *do* mind," I said. "I'm busy too. Maybe if you would organize your time better, you wouldn't be running late." To top it off, he had 14 items, not 12. I didn't mean to snap at him, but I've felt so exhausted and irritable lately. Being a mother and father to Robby and bread winner since Jeff died two years ago hasn't been easy.

October 6, 1973. Today I had a teacher interview with Robby's third grade teacher, Mr. Corrigan, who is new at the school this year. As I walked into the room for my interview, my jaw dropped. The man at the check out counter! "Mrs. Andrews," he said, extending his hand, "I'm Paul Corrigan. It's nice to meet you under more pleasant circumstances. Sorry about last night." His lively blue eyes twinkled and a smile spread across his face as if he were enjoying a private joke. After my initial embarrassment, he soon put me at ease.

Sandra flipped the journal pages ahead and wiped her eyes.

November 28, 1973. Tonight I was at choir practice, the one activity I allow myself on a weekday evening. In came Paul Corrigan. Imagine that! I noticed him in church the past two Sundays.

February 16, 1974. Paul Corrigan is certainly an interesting man. Intriguing! Fascinating! What more can I say? I wonder why he is still single.

May 4, 1974. Lord, am I imagining things? As Paul and I spend more time together, it seems like You brought him into my life. I admire his vibrant faith, after all he's been through—losing his mother at the age of 12, losing a younger brother a couple years later from an asthma attack. I think I'm falling in love. I didn't think I could love anyone else after losing Jeff.

August 10, 1974. A full moon reflected on the glass-like surface of the lake tonight. My thumping heart was drowning out the sound of the crickets as I sat on the park bench. Then, with a dramatic flourish, Paul got down on one knee and took my hands in his (and almost lost his balance—I giggled). "Sandra Andrews," he solemnly said, "I love you more than I've dreamed possible. Will you marry me?" "Yes! Yes! Yes!"

March 18, 1975. Does anyone have a right to be this outrageously, deliriously happy? At 2 p.m. today, in front of family and a few close friends, Paul and I will say our vows. Sandra Corrigan has a nice ring to it. And Robby is delighted to have Paul for his new dad.

October 24, 1976. This is one of the hardest days of my life. Little Rebecca was born at 3:15 a.m. six weeks premature — a dusky gray, not a healthy pink. The doctors said her heart hadn't developed correctly. I held her limp little body as life slipped away four hours later. I know I'll see her in heaven, but letting go is hard . . . so very hard. Paul put his arms around me. "This didn't take God by surprise," he said gently and let me sob on his shoulder. "He understands our pain." Our tears mingled together.

July 14, 1978. Thank you, Lord, for a beautiful, healthy baby girl. No heart problem this time. Jennifer Lynn was born at 5:30 this morning. I already know she has a healthy set of lungs. Rob, who is now 13, said he would rather have a brother, but a sister will do.

FICTION

October 15, 1982. Paul and I went to the big Central High football game tonight. Rob was a starter. We were so proud of him. Then in the third quarter, a tackle on the opposing team—at least 6"4" and 230 pounds — mauled him. He didn't have a chance. He was down on the ground so long, not moving. A doctor from the stands checked him over for a spinal cord injury and possible concussion. Dear Lord, I'm so scared. Will Rob ever walk again? Paul and I spent the night sitting in the waiting room by the intensive care unit, visiting Rob five minutes each hour. Friends and members of our church were praying.

October 18, 1982. Rob is now conscious and is getting feeling back into his arms and legs. Doctors feel he will eventually make a complete recovery, although the football season is over for him. Lord, I know You were there with us and brought us through this difficult time.

Sandra glanced at her watch and grabbed another tissue. Since time was passing quickly, she grabbed a recent journal.

March 18, 2000. Today is our 25th wedding anniversary—25 wonderful years of being married to a wonderful man. I couldn't be happier! What more could I ask for? We drove up to Jasper to enjoy the majestic scenery, and stayed in a romantic little lodge. Paul turned 60 in February and is retiring after serving as a elementary school principal the past 17 years. He still loves children, but now needs time to do all of the things he hasn't had time to do. This summer he will be turning his job over to a new principal and working with him during a transition time. We're starting to make plans for our future.

July 30, 2000. What a beautiful bride Jen was today. How proud Paul and I are! Of course we were happy when Rob got married eight years ago, but somehow a daughter getting married is different. She's following in her father's footsteps. She graduated from university with a teaching degree and has a job starting this fall. David is a wonderful man, and I'm fully confident he will make a good husband.

October 20, 2000. Paul hasn't been feeling well lately. He says it's only indigestion, but I'm feeling concerned. It's not at all like Paul to get indigestion.

November 18, 2000. Paul experienced more stomach pains and other symptoms. He had tests done two weeks ago, the results were back today. Cancer. The big C. And it's widespread. Doctors will do surgery, but hold out no promises. I feel angry. Why this? Why now? Why us? God, why has this happened?

January 3, 2001. After removing several tumors in December, the doctors are starting Paul on chemo. They can't promise any miracles, only that it will buy a little time. What is time? We never give it any thought, and don't appreciate it until it slips through our fingers. It reminds me of Psalm 135: "Our times are in Your hands." Only God knows how much Paul has. The doctors don't. I don't. Only God, and He's not telling us. Of course we're praying for healing, but face the very real possibility that God's answer is "no."

February 18, 2001. Today is Paul's 61st birthday. Jen and David came over, and so did Rob, Karen and their two children. Paul was weak but happy. He had chemo three days ago and it made him sick, so he's had difficulty eating. But he enjoyed having his family around him. Little things mean so much now days.

April 23, 2001. I am unable to care for Paul at home any longer. What a difficult decision! Today Jen, David and I took him to the hospice where he is surrounded by caring staff. Paul motioned for me to come close to him. "I'm looking forward to a home . . . which needs no repairs . . . and has no lawn to mow." His voice was barely audible, but the twinkle was still in his blue eyes. He is ready to meet his Lord, but am I ready to let him go?

The journal stopped on that day. Sandra died her eyes and threw a handful of soggy tissues into a nearby waste basket. Then she got a pen from the desk drawer and in bold strokes dated a new page, leaving a few blank pages in between. She would go back and fill them in later.

May 5, 2001. Dear God, thank you for the wonderful years Paul and I had together. He was a wonderful husband and I miss him so very much. I know he is with You. I know You will be with me like You have been in all of the difficult times in the past. Even in the times when I can't feel Your presence—there will be plenty of those in the days to come—I know You are with me. Amen.

Sandra closed the journal and put it on her desk. The older journals she stacked carefully in the storage box. Then she walked to the bathroom, washed her face and reapplied her makeup. Her two hours were up.

When the doorbell rang, she opened the door and greeted Jen with a hug. "Are you ready?" asked Jen. Her eyes had a hint of red from crying. "David will be meeting us at the funeral home."

"Yes," said Sandra softly. "Now I'm ready."

A Rainbow for Jenny

Kate gazed wearily at the stacks of packing boxes cluttering the room. She had lived in Australia all of her life, but moving to Darwin was like moving to a different world. The Top End of Down Under, they called it. More like the End of Civilization—"Crocodile Dundee" country, to be sure. Only she hadn't seen a water buffalo or a crocodile yet. Would she ever feel at home up here? she wondered. For that matter, would anywhere feel like home again?

She pulled a calendar out of the box she was unpacking, and flipped the pages to May 1986. Her world had died three pages before that. She still felt numb.

"Mum, can I wear this?" asked eight-year-old Meagan. She triumphantly waved a shirt that she had retrieved from one of the boxes. "It's been lost, and I only just found it." In the process, she had knocked another box to the floor, spilling the contents.

Kate winced as she felt a fresh stab of pain. The mess on the floor didn't bother her as much as the shirt Meagan was holding. "I wish you wouldn't wear that one yet."

"Why not? This rainbow shirt from my Nanna is my favorite. Besides, it was Jenny's favorite too."

"It reminds me too much of Jenny right now, dear." In fact, Kate thought, Jenny was wearing her matching rainbow shirt the night of the accident.

"Don't you want to remember Jenny?" Meagan's dark eyes flashed with anger and pain. Then, when she saw the hurt expression on her mother's face, her voice softened. "Mum, if God loved Jenny, why did He let her die?"

Why indeed? thought Kate angrily. "I don't know, Meagan," she responded, with a sharpness to her voice she hadn't meant. "Now please go outside and play and let me unpack in peace."

After she heard the back door close, Kate was sorry she had been so abrupt with her daughter. She should

FICTION

have been reaching out to comfort her instead of sending her away. What bothered her most was Meagan's questions echoed the ones which had been running through her own mind—questions which had no answers.

She could hear her husband Roger rummaging around in the room he claimed as his office. His grief had been private, and he covered his hurt by throwing himself into his work. The transfer from Sydney to Darwin had looked good to him. It would give them a chance to start over again, he had said. Kate had agreed with him, but now that she was actually in Darwin, she wasn't so sure. Darwin was in the middle of nowhere and had only 70,000 people—not at all like the city where Kate grew up.

Kate wiped the cupboard shelves and tackled her next task—the boxes marked "kitchen cupboard." While she was removing some of the items from one of the boxes, she picked up a rainbow refrigerator magnet—a Christmas present from Jenny. Her mind drifted back to a time a little more than three months ago when her world was still whole.

She could picture bubbly six-year-old Jenny—their "Rainbow Girl," they called her—with her rainbow shirt and rainbow ribbons tying her dark hair into two pony tails. Rainbows were the fad of the time, and Jenny had rainbow stickers on her books, a rainbow poster on the wall, a rainbow bedspread, and she had even insisted on having a rainbow cake for her last birthday. People said rainbows were New Age, but Kate always maintained that rainbows were God's invention in the first place.

"Jenny, dear Jenny. Why did you leave us so soon?" Kate whispered, tears welling up in her eyes.

Then Kate's mind shifted to the tragic night branded forever on her memory. It was like one of those continuous tape loops which play over and over again: The squeal of tires; Meagan running in the front door, screaming; the wail of the ambulance. Uniformed men gently lifting Jenny's bleeding body from where she lay beside her mangled bicycle.

Kate grabbed a tissue and dabbed at her eyes. "God, why did You seem so far away when I needed You?" she questioned, remembering the anxious waiting for Jenny to come out of the operating theater; the grim-faced doctors; three long days and nights of not knowing if Jenny would live or die. She and Roger prayed, their church prayed, all of their friends prayed. And then the doctor turned off the life support.

"Love, please come here for a minute." Roger's voice broke into Kate's thoughts and abruptly jarred her back to the present. "Do you remember how you marked the box with all of my computer books? I can't seem to locate it."

Weeks turned into months and Kate felt no more at home in Darwin than when she first arrived. There were just two seasons—wet and dry—and they were both equally oppressive. By July, the dry season had turned the landscape into a dusty brown, and every blade of grass and every plant that wasn't carefully watered, withered and died. The weather wasn't as hot as wet season, but not a drop of rain would fall until November.

The house where Kate and Roger were living was in the country, but construction seemed to be going on all around them as the city edged outward. Across the road workmen were beginning excavation for a new building and the earth-moving equipment cut a gaping wound in the red earth. Huge trucks sent piles of red dust billowing into the air, drifting into their house, settling on the louvered windows and the furniture, grinding underfoot on the tile floor. Kate could even taste it. She vacuumed, scrubbed, mopped and dusted to no avail. Country living at it's very best, she thought ruefully. As if the dust wasn't bad enough, often grass fires filled the air with acrid smoke which stung Kate's eyes and nose.

Several application forms for relief teaching positions were still stacked in a pile on her desk where she had put them a number of weeks earlier. She had greatly enjoyed teaching in Sydney, but that was "before" and this was "af-

FICTION

ter." Her whole life seemed to be divided into "before" and "after." How could she deal with her classroom full of children when she was still having trouble coping? They could survive without her paycheck, so Roger encouraged her to wait until she was ready . . . maybe when the new term started in January.

Gardening was one of her favorite hobbies in Sydney and her flowers had even won prizes in local competitions, so Kate planted a garden, thinking it would make her feel more at home. However, the scorching tropical sun beat down relentlessly, drying up the tender seedlings almost before they came out of the ground. Even watering them morning and night didn't help.

Doesn't anything grow up here? Kate thought angrily, ignoring the fact that her neighbors had luxurious growths of tropical shrubs in their yards.

Kate did find an occasional bright spot in her days when she visited her neighbor Ruth. One day as they sat drinking lemonade on Ruth's verandah, Kate turned to the kindly silver-haired woman beside her and asked, "Ruth, how did you get over your son's death after the motorcycle accident? But don't tell me that time heals because I've heard that all before."

There was a momentary sadness reflected in Ruth's blue eyes as she paused and thoughtfully wiped her glasses with her handkerchief. "You've got to remember that John's death was a long time ago. Your grief is fresh. As time passes, the pain will get bearable, but it never fully goes away. Birthdays and Christmas are especially difficult." Then Ruth turned and looked at Kate meaningfully. "Whatever you do, Kate, don't live in the past. It won't bring Jenny back, and it's not fair to Roger or Meagan. You've got to keep on living in the present. God gives you only the grace to live one day at a time. You can't store it up from day to day."

The pages of the calendar slipped past one by one; the sky had been a cloudless blue for months, but now clouds formed and went scudding past. Occasional light showers provided no relief and only increased the humidity.

Kate had heard people talk about the "the build up to the wet" and thought they were exaggerating. Now she knew it was no joke. Day after day her damp clothes stuck to her body and her dark hair hung limply around her face. No matter how many showers she took each day, she always felt hot and uncomfortable.

Roger came home irritable at night. Meagan, who was usually good-natured, whined for no reason at all. Kate found it a real effort to be civil.

Then one day she heard a rumble off in the distance. As the thunder and lightning gradually came closer, the sky turned inky black and wept great tears which bathed the parched earth and washed over the fire-charred grasslands. Water ran in rivulets across the footpaths and filled the gully across the road with a gushing torrent. Even the smell of dust was gone from the air. Healing had come to the land.

Kate marveled at the new green shoots which began poking through the dead grass and was surprised to find pink, white and green Caladium leaves unfurling like little flags all over the garden in front of the house. The bulbs had been dormant during the dry season, and Kate hadn't even realized they were there.

Several sulfur-crested cockatoos flew into the yard to drink from a water puddle; in a nearby gum tree a pair of kookaburras filled the air with their raucous laughter. Each day was filled with new surprises.

On her way home from school one afternoon, Meagan brought home a large green frog which had taken up residence in the gully. It had suction pads on its feet, and when Meagan put it on the outside of the house, it began climbing straight up and made Kate laugh. Then she realized it was the first time she had laughed in a long time. It was good to find simple joy again—to feel like living again instead of merely existing.

Then one evening as Kate was reading the newspaper, Meagan burst into the room, bubbling with excitement. "Mum, come with me!"

Kate looked up. "You're all wet! Were you out in the rain?"

"The rain's stopped now, and there's something you just have to see." Meagan danced a jig around her mother until Kate eased herself from the chair. The two of them went out the back door.

There, arched over the field behind their house, was one of the brightest rainbows Kate had ever seen. In fact, when she looked carefully, she could see it was a double rainbow with a second faint bow around the first.

"A rainbow for Jenny," Meagan said impulsively and then stopped abruptly, looking at her mother to see her reaction.

Kate noticed that for the first time those words didn't feel like a knife twisting in her heart. God's grace was working in her life.

"Yes, I'm sure Jenny would have loved it," she said, turning to Meagan and smiling. They stood watching until the rainbow at last began to fade.

"A rainbow for Jenny," Kate whispered softly as she put her arm around her daughter and the two of them walked into the house.

This won first prize in InScribe Christian Writers' Fellowship fiction division in 1999.

Next Exit Grapevine

A few downy snowflakes floated down as Sandra Morris retrieved a hamburger wrapper and her son Brett's overdue library book from the back seat of the old blue Ford. Then she carefully put her suitcase in the trunk. She was looking forward to this weekend in Dallas in more ways than one.

When was the last time she had been away from home for a weekend? She couldn't remember. It seemed like she and Greg never went out any more, and family vacations were a thing of the past since Greg went into business for himself four years ago.

"Sandra, I'm glad you'll be able to get away." Her friend Carol, standing near the car, interrupted her thoughts. "The break will do you good."

Sandra shut the trunk and looked up. "I've been saving for this for a long time. And thanks so much for watching Melanie. She'll be home from school at 3:30. Brett will be going home with his friend David directly after school."

"Watching Melanie will be no problem. After all, what are friends for if they can't help each other?" replied Carol cheerfully. "I know how much this writers' convention means to you."

"I left a note for Greg along with the hotel phone number," added Sandra as she slid behind the wheel. "He'll probably be working late again and won't even remember I'm going to Dallas this weekend." She gave a rueful laugh.

"At least you still have a husband and know where he is," Carol reminded her. The irony of Carol's words gave a little tug at Sandra's heart. Had Carol guessed there was something more than just a convention to draw her to Dallas?

With a quick wave, Sandra shut the door, buckled her seat belt, and turned the key in the ignition. By starting out at 2 p.m. she would avoid the rush hour traffic in Oklahoma City where she lived. The 180-mile drive south should go

FICTION

smoothly since highway 35 was in good condition. Although it was the first weekend in December, the weather was still pleasant.

The congestion of city traffic soon gave way to intermittent trees and shrubs. Occasionally farms and small towns dotted the landscape, and of course the ever-present oil wells.

As the heater warmed the car, Sandra slipped off her jacket and then turned on the radio to keep her company. She pushed back the dark curls which framed her face and made her look younger than her 35 years.

Yes, she had been looking forward to this weekend at the Dallas Writers' Convention for a long time. The money for the convention came from what she had been able to save from working part time at Dawson's Bookstore.

She thought back to how writing had been a hobby at first until she had sold some of her articles. Now it was a passion with her and she looked forward to meeting some editors.

And then there was Kevin. . . .

When had she first met him? About 10 months ago? Her thoughts drifted back to the first time he had walked into the bookstore. Kevin was the regional representative for the Ace Office Supplies company based in Dallas, Texas, and had been given Oklahoma as part of his territory. Although Dawson's Bookstore in Oklahoma City carried mainly books, it could boast of a well-stocked office supply section. It was Kevin's job to make sure their office supply needs were met.

Kevin was in his early 40s, had wavy dark hair which was graying at the temples, and blue eyes which danced when he talked. With a Texas drawl and a booming laugh, his presence seemed to light up the whole room.

Over the months he had been stopping at the store, Sandra began to look forward to his visits. She learned that he was divorced and that his 17-year-old son lived with his ex-wife. He, in turn, knew about Sandra's athletic 13-year-old son Brett and about her bubbly, good-natured 10-year-old daughter Melanie. He had seen their photos on her desk and asked about them. But Sandra had never mentioned Greg; there had never been any reason to do so.

An avid reader, Kevin had seen some of Sandra's articles in a local magazine and had showered her with praise for her writing ability. Why did his compliments mean so much more than Greg's? Not that she got many compliments from Greg anymore. In November, as he was leaving the store, Kevin spotted the writers' convention poster that Sandra had stuck up on the bulletin board.

"Hey, that's in Dallas, my stompin' grounds. Are you planning to go?" A broad smile lit up Kevin's handsome face.

"Yes. I'm really looking forward to it. Friends in Dallas highly recommended it."

"They usually don't keep you busy the first couple hours of those things—just serve snacks, hand out name tags, and get acquainted. Why don't you give me a call. Here's my number in Grapevine, on the north edge of Dallas. I'd love to show you some of the sights of the city."

He fixed his gaze meaningfully on Sandra as she signed the purchase order for the office supplies she was ordering. "Have you ever seen the Dallas skyline at night? It's marvelous from Reunion Tower. The food there is great too." Sandra was stunned.

Kevin's eyes twinkled as he continued, "I'm serious about the invitation. Think it over and let me know."

What could she say? "No thanks, I'm married." Those words just wouldn't come, even if she had wanted to say them. She just smiled numbly and said, "Sounds like fun."

At first Sandra couldn't believe the conversation she had just had with Kevin. Kevin had always been completely honest in his dealings with the store—straight as an arrow, as she put it. He was a man of integrity, unlike most of the salesmen she had met. It was totally out of character for him to try to date a married woman. Then slowly the truth began to dawn on Sandra: "He thinks I'm divorced too!"

FICTION

True, she had never given him any indication that she was divorced, but then she was not wearing her wedding ring. Because of a persistent case of dermatitis, she had taken off her ring months ago. It was not her intention to deceive him, but she had unwittingly done so, and had done nothing to correct the misunderstanding.

At first Sandra pushed all thoughts of Kevin from her mind, but later they persisted in creeping back. Then in her unhappiness with Greg, she began to imagine spending an evening with Kevin. Temptation reared its ugly head, and she did nothing to flee it. Like seeds planted on fertile ground, those thoughts had flourished and were about to bear fruit. Now in less than two hours she was going to meet Kevin. Just this one time. No one would know. No one would be hurt.

The miles rolled by and the gas gauge was registering a quarter of a tank when she took the exit to Addison, just over the Oklahoma-Texas border, and pulled into a gas station. Nice little town. How could she forget? Addison was where she and Greg had spent the night 15 years ago sleeping in their parked car in a rainstorm. . . all because of a broken water hose at 10 p.m. It was in the early days of their marriage—and they were so broke they couldn't afford a hotel. It wasn't funny at the time, but later it became a family joke.

After Sandra paid the service station attendant, her thoughts drifted back to Greg in Oklahoma City. What would he be doing tonight? No doubt he would stay in his office until 9 p.m. as he often did on Friday nights. He poured all his time, energy, and their life savings into the computer business he had started four years ago, and it still wasn't much of a money-making proposition. Would it ever be? He was more married to his work than he was to her.

Funny, that was one of the things she had admired about him when she met him and fell in love with him while they were both attending the University of Oklahoma—his hard work. They had married in her junior year and she dropped out so she could put him through school and he could complete his degree.

Greg was always looking for new challenges. That was another of the things she had admired about him. Well, she needed challenges and broader horizons too. That's why a writing course in night school two years ago was so important to her; it had opened up a whole new world to her. Her job at the bookstore soon after that had given her an opportunity to meet new and interesting people . . . like Kevin.

Traffic was getting heavier now as Sandra got nearer Dallas. In 20 miles she would be coming to an exit marked Grapevine, the one Kevin had told her to take to meet him. Far more than an exit on the highway, Grapevine was also symbolic of a fork in her life. She knew if she took it, nothing would ever be quite the same.

Saying that no one would ever know wasn't quite the truth and Sandra knew it. "Just this one time" was probably also a lie. And lies get easier the second and third time around.

Was this really what she wanted? Suddenly her fantastic plans for a special evening didn't seem so fantastic anymore.

Nervously she reached over and switched stations on the radio. She had been so lost in her thoughts for most of the trip that she had barely noticed when the background music had changed to static.

Now she recognized a few Christmas songs the new station was playing, and one caught her attention. "There's no place like home for the holidays." That song was really an "oldie but goody" as Greg would say. She found herself humming along.

"Home for the holidays. . ." A wave of nostalgia hit her, as she remembered all of the Christmases they had spent together as a family. . . gathered around the Christmas tree, singing songs at the piano, reading the Christmas story, opening presents, going to the candlelight Christmas eve service at church—times of fun and laughter she would always treasure.

FICTION

Suddenly memories flooded back of other times spent together: of birthdays, a special family vacation, taking turns walking the floor with Brett when he was cutting teeth, sitting at the bedside of Melanie, in the hospital with pneumonia, as she struggled to breathe. It was Greg's strength she had leaned on, Greg who was part of all of those memories.

They were still a family . . . she and Greg and Brett and Melanie. The invisible glue of shared experiences held them all together. True, there had been difficult times lately, but no different from what most families go through at one time or another. A few tears slid down Sandra's cheeks and she brushed them away.

The exit to Grapevine was coming up immediately on her right, and she needed to make a decision. Which would it be? She couldn't have it both ways.

With firm resolve, she held the wheel steady and drove right past.

Now she knew exactly what she would do. When she got to her hotel in downtown Dallas, she would make two phone calls—one to Kevin, to tell him the truth, and the other to Greg at his office, to tell him how much she still loved him.

Just then the setting sun lit up the sky with glorious pinks and golds and outlined the tall buildings of downtown Dallas off in the distance. It was far more beautiful to her than a thousand Dallas skylines seen from the top of Reunion Tower with Kevin.

Sarah, Please Come Home

Groggy from sleep, Cheryl was awakened by persistent ringing. *Who on earth is ringing the doorbell at this hour?* She fearfully glanced at the clock—1:25 a.m. She decided not to awaken her paramedic husband, Rick, since he had an early morning shift.

From the kitchen window, she saw flashing lights of a police car.

"Mrs. Anderson," the officer confronted her at the door, "we have your daughter and two of her friends in the car."

"There must be some mistake," she responded, shivering in the April night air. "Sarah and her friends are having a sleepover in our basement. They were eating popcorn when my husband and I went to bed."

"Apparently they had something to drink with their popcorn," the officer continued, "because they are quite drunk. We caught them ringing doorbells a couple blocks from here. Someone phoned 911."

"I don't understand. We don't even have alcohol in the house." *Things like this don't happen to Christian families—do they*? she thought.

That was just the beginning. Soon Cheryl noticed other changes in their once vibrant and cooperative 16-year-old. Grades began slipping. Although Sarah had accepted the Lord as a youngster, she now refused to go church. An empty cigarette packet showed up in her jacket pocket. Every conversation seemed to end in an argument.

This room looks like a pig sty, thought Cheryl one day, shoving Sarah's door open. As she set a stack of clean clothes on Sarah's bed, her foot bumped something hard under the bed. Shock spread through her as she picked up an empty rum bottle.

Discipline didn't work. It was as if Sarah dared them to punish her—the more the better.

Things came to a crisis in September. One Friday night

FICTION

when Sarah came home hours after her curfew, it was obvious she had been drinking.

The next morning Rick angrily confronted her. "No drinking, Sarah! We already told you that. If you live in our house, you'll live by our rules."

Sarah swore softly. "Then I'm out of here." With that she stomped into her room and threw a few belongings into a backpack. "Don't bother looking for me. I don't live here anymore!" she shouted. The back door slammed loudly behind her.

Cheryl and Rick stood there in shock.

She won't go very far, they reasoned, especially since she has almost no money. When she hadn't returned by evening, Cheryl began calling a list of Sarah's friends. No one knew where she was.

The next day Rick and Cheryl went to the police station. When the officer finished filling out the form, he turned to them. "Abduction cases are different. We deal with them. Your daughter is a runaway. If we searched for every runaway here in the city, we'd have no time to do anything else. We'll let you know if we see her."

On that somber note Sarah became a statistic—one more runaway.

That night Cheryl sobbed as Rick held her in his arms. "We've got to remember that the Lord loves her even more than we do," he said. "This hasn't caught Him by surprise. We have to learn to trust Him." But trusting was easier said than done.

Days passed, and she didn't come back. They called her friends again. Together Rick and Cheryl visited several homeless shelters and showed the staff Sarah's photo. No one had seen her.

Early one morning Rick was on duty when his ambulance answered a 911 call to pick up an assault victim in the downtown area. The young blonde girl—about Sarah's age and height—had been badly beaten. Was she a prostitute living on the street? Rick was ashen as he turned away from the sight, and fought for control. Thank God it wasn't Sarah—but it might have been.

They finally located a friend of Sarah's who had talked with her recently. They marked the date on the calendar.

Sometimes Cheryl felt angry, sometimes numb; at other times fear was a lion, crouching in the corner, ready to pounce on her and devour her.

One sunny October afternoon Cheryl walked to her special place of refuge in a park two blocks from home, a favorite family picnic area when Sarah and her brother were younger. Today Cheryl came to think and to pray. Sitting on a bench, she watched golden autumn leaves drop one by one and noticed geese overhead in their familiar v formation. *They know which way to fly for the winter,* she thought. *Too bad my daughter doesn't have the same homing instinct.*

"Lord," she prayed, "we miss Sarah so much." Then her prayer switched to asking "Why?" She thought of Sarah, their lovely daughter who was everyone's friend. What had changed this? It was a time of soul-searching. What could they have done differently?

But God was silent, and that silence was deafening.

She and Rick noticed some of their friends subtly avoided them. *Are they afraid that having a runaway child is contagious?* Cheryl wondered angrily. The hardest blow came when Carol, a friend from church, quoted Scripture and said, "You brought this on yourself, Cheryl. You shouldn't have sent Sarah to that public school, and you should have known what kind of friends she had."

Cheryl was shocked—and then she realized how smug she herself had been in the past, comparing her *good* children with others who were rebellious. Her thoughts drifted to Sarah constantly, making it difficult to concentrate on her secretarial job. *Where is Sarah living? What is she doing? Is she a prostitute? Does she have AIDS? Is she pregnant? On drugs?*

FICTION

Once Cheryl might have rejected a pregnant daughter, but now she would welcome her home. She was learning about grace—God's grace, and it was *such a painful lesson.*

Just before Christmas, the phone rang. Cheryl's heart raced as she heard Sarah's voice.

"Mom, it's me. I'm fine." Sarah blurted out the words.

"Honey, please come home," Cheryl begged. "We love you."

"Bye," was the abrupt response.

Sarah's presents under the tree remained untouched, and the season was filled with sadness.

The door of Sarah's room remained shut, but several times Cheryl ventured in and sat on the bed, thinking and praying. Sarah's school sweatshirt hung in the closet and several of her sports medals hung on her bulletin board. She had been so proud of Sarah's accomplishments on the swim team and in track.

We did everything we could to help her get ahead, Cheryl thought, dabbing her eyes with a tissue. *She had so much potential. Now she's thrown it all away.* Then a new thought struck her, *Did we ever ask Sarah what she wanted to do with her life? Did we ever really listen to her? Or were we too busy giving advice?*

Months slipped by and the days grew longer. A few more people had talked with Sarah, confirming she was still in the city.

Years ago Cheryl had memorized the verse Proverbs 22:6 (NIV):"Train a child in the way he should go, and when he is old he will not turn from it." Now those words became a lifeline. She was learning to trust her Lord in a way she had never done before. Sarah was in His hands, and so was she.

One Saturday in April the trees were beginning to bud, a damp, earthy smell filled the air, and Cheryl noticed tulips poking their heads up in her garden. The long, harsh winter was ending.

This spring day is too beautiful to waste, she thought as she walked down to her favorite place in the park. As she sat on the bench, she could hear birds warbling in the trees. Easter was a week away, and the week beyond that was Sarah's 17th birthday. As she thanked God for the beauty of the day, a feeling of peace settled over her.

Suddenly, she heard a squish of soggy dead leaves behind the park bench. Startled, she whirled around to see where the sound had come from and found herself face to face with Sarah. Her greasy blond hair hung limply around her shoulders, and she was thinner than last fall.

"Dad said I would find you here," Sarah mumbled with eyes downcast as she shifted the backpack on her shoulder. "I miss the old times. I want to come home."

Emotion welled up within Cheryl, but she stifled the impulse to jump up and hug this stranger. There would be time for that later. "Welcome home," she said gently.

FICTION

Our Times Are in Your Hands

Blinking lights on the small Christmas tree reflected off the blue and red balls, reminding Kelly Goodwin of childhood Christmases. Outside huge snowflakes were floating down, turning the world into a winter wonderland. This was her fifth Christmas with her husband, David. *How quickly time passes*, she thought.

Leaning back in her reclining chair, she welcomed a rare moment to relax on this Sunday afternoon. What a mad, mad Christmas rush!

Tomorrow night at Oak Ridge Elementary School her third graders would be performing for their parents in the Winter Festival program. After that, she still had most of her Christmas shopping to do and preparation for her part in the annual family Christmas celebration—for as many as 30 people. When would this insanity end?

Without thinking, she picked up "Reaching Beyond," a denominational newsletter, from the end table next to her chair. As she began thumbing through it, an article caught her attention. "David," she said, turning to her husband, "listen to this."

David, who was reading his latest John Grisham novel, looked up from his book.

"They need teachers in the school for missionary kids in Kenya. It says specifically that they need a teacher for a combination third and fourth grade class for two years. I could do that."

She knew she had David's full attention when she mentioned Kenya, since David had lived in Africa for several years when he was growing up.

"Before we were married we talked about doing missionary work. Remember?" she continued. "It would be fantastic to teach in a Christian school where I could actually teach about Christmas—and not call it a Winter Festival."

"Do they need an experienced computer programmer?" David asked.

"This article is about the need for teachers, but I'm sure they need computer personnel too. Most mission organizations do." Kelly was already heading toward their computer to search for the website listed in the article.

"Let's pray about this over Christmas," David replied. "I've always wanted to return to Africa some day. Maybe next Christmas we can use a banana tree for our Christmas tree and I wouldn't need to shovel our driveway." He was grinning broadly.

After the Christmas holidays, they sought out Pastor Gary Stanford, who was the missions pastor at Riverside Church. He was delighted to hear their thoughts.

"I've had an interest in missions since I was a teenager and David's parents worked in Cameroon for three years when he was in grade school," said Kelly. "We're thinking that now would be a good time to go overseas before we have children or become too settled in our careers and suburban living."

"Good thinking." Pastor Gary nodded.

"There's one problem. We need to raise our own support. We've never done anything like that other than for a summer missions trip," confided Kelly. "Quite frankly, it scares me."

"Others have done it successfully, so I'm sure you can do it too." Pastor Gary was thoughtful. "I'll give you what encouragement I can. I know that Riverside Church has money set aside for short term work, and you can apply for that."

"We'd be very grateful for Riverside's support," said David.

"You'll also need to let your friends know what you are planning to do so they can come on board as prayer and financial partners."

When she got home from church, Kelly got out a new 1998 calendar and started making a time line. She wrote down things they needed to do: get passports renewed, obtain a Kenyan visa, interview with the mission director, vaccinations, find someone to rent their house, make plane reservations.

Things moved rapidly, and friends soon got excited. Financial pledges rolled in and they moved forward in their planning. It was obvious to them that God was leading and directing.

One Saturday morning in May, Kelly visited with her older sister, Brenda, over a cup of coffee. Brenda and her husband, John, lived in an area near the University of Minnesota where he taught English.

"Wow! A two-year commitment? You've never done anything more adventurous than working with migrant children in California for two weeks in the summer." Brenda took a sip of her coffee as she watched her two preschoolers at play in their fenced-in yard. "Are you sure you can handle two years?"

"If God is calling us, He will provide whatever we need," said Kelly with assurance. She had seen God provide in numerous ways before, including getting through school nearly debt free with some fantastic scholarships.

"What are you planning to do with all of your household items while you're away?" asked Brenda, always one to be practical.

"We'll put our personal things into a basement room which we'll lock, and then find a Christian family to rent our furnished house."

"If you need somewhere to stay between the time the house is rented and when you actually get on the plane, you can live in our little apartment above our garage," Brenda offered. "While John was in grad school, we supplemented our income by renting it to students. Now that he's teaching, we have a steady income."

"That would be great! Thanks for your offer." Kelly smiled, thankful that her sister—even though she wasn't always enthusiastic in the beginning—always came through for her in the end.

Kelly resigned her teaching position for the fall, and David eased back on his work until he was exclusively doing freelance projects. Pledges for funding continued to come in.

They booked their tickets in mid-July for the flights on September 2. They would be taking Northwest Airlines from Minneapolis to New York, Swissair from New York to Geneva, Switzerland, and then transferring to another Swissair flight the rest of the way to Kenya. Unfortunately, there was no direct route.

One Sunday Pastor Gary saw them in the church hallway. "I know you have been praying about someone to stay in your house. Friends of mine from Chicago have been transferred here for two years and will be arriving the end of July. They're looking for a house to rent and can provide references."

"That's awesome," said David, "I can't believe how God is answering our prayers. It's apparent that the Lord wants us in Africa because everything has been falling into place."

In July, when the Masons arrived to live in their house, David and Kelly moved into John and Brenda's apartment. It was tiny but comfortable with a combination living room and kitchenette, a bedroom and a bathroom.

Then something strange happened. No more pledges came in, and elderly Mrs. Wilcox, a wealthy widow who had offered to give them $150 each month, died unexpectedly of a heart attack. Not only had they come to a standstill, they were now moving backward!

Dr. Brandon, the director of the mission they were joining, phoned them to talk over the situation. "Up until now you've been making great progress. However, we require you to have 100 percent of the money pledged, and you're now at 65 percent. If you don't have your full support before the date of your flight, you won't be able to leave for Kenya." Dr. Brandon was kind but firm. "We've found that people who come with less than full support usually have financial problems on the field."

FICTION

The thought was sobering. What could they do? Their flight was booked; someone else was living in their house. They both had given up their jobs, and now they were looking ahead at the prospect of not going when they planned. Or maybe not going at all unless something happened with their support level.

A few days later, they spread their problems before the mission pastor at church.

"Pastor Gary, what is God trying to tell us? We were so sure we were following His will. Now everything seems to be falling apart," said Kelly, emotional strain showing on her face.

Pastor Gary was thoughtful. "Sometimes things happen that don't make sense to us this side of heaven. We'll understand later on, but not now. I'm sure the steps you've taken are God's will for you. You wanted to serve Him and have stepped out in faith."

He paused a minute and then went on, "Sometimes God's timetable isn't the same as ours. Psalm 31:15 says, "Our times are in His hands." I think for now He just wants you to trust Him even though you can't see where or how He is leading at the moment."

Their flight would be on September 2 and there was no way they would be going. Not unless God worked a miracle. They were standing on the bank of their Red Sea, and the waters weren't about to part. On August 30, they sadly cancelled their tickets, hoping it wouldn't be too much of a hassle to get their money back.

On September 1, Kelly took a walk along East River Road near Brenda's house. She had taken that route many times during her year at the university before transferring to Bethel College where she had met David. She knew a quiet place along the river under the protective arch of some willow trees. In the past she had often come there to think and pray.

An autumn chill was in the air as she settled down under the willows and watched the sunlight play on the water. A few yellow leaves fell into the rushing river and were swept away.

"Lord," she poured her heart out, "It doesn't make sense. It just doesn't make sense at all. We're trying so hard to be obedient and we stepped out in faith. School will be starting here in a few days, and I no longer have my class at Oak Ridge Elementary School. We no longer have our house to live in. David no longer has his job. I know you tell us that all things work together for good in Romans 8:28. People have reminded me of that a lot lately." She took out a tissue and wiped her eyes. "Help me trust You, Lord."

The night of September 2, David and Kelly went to bed, but didn't sleep well. They would have been flying that day, but of course all of the flights had left without them. What would they do next?

Early the next morning someone was pounding on their door. "It must be Brenda, but why would she be knocking on our door at this hour?" Kelly wondered aloud as she slipped on her robe.

Ashen faced, Brenda gripped the morning newspaper in her hands. "Have you heard the news?"

"No, we haven't had the T.V. on," Kelly said sleepily, stifling a yawn. "What's wrong?"

Then Kelly looked at the paper Brenda thrust at her. The headlines screamed at her "229 killed in Swissair crash off Nova Scotia."

She continued reading: "As the sun rose over the Atlantic Ocean Thursday, hopes for finding survivors from the crash of Swissair Flight 111 dimmed, as airline officials said they believed all 229 people aboard the aircraft had died.

"As of daylight, 18 bodies had been recovered, officials said. A flotilla of search crews was canvassing the waters off Peggy's Cove, a popular tourist destination."

As the news settled in slowly, a sob escaped from Kelly. "That was the flight we would have been on," she said. "The Lord was really watching over us. We just didn't understand it at the time."

After Brenda left, David came over and put his arms around Kelly. Then they quietly sat on the edge of the bed.

"Lord, thank you for keeping us safe," David prayed. "Thank you for knowing what was best for us. Our times really are in Your Hands."

Based on a true story. All characters are fictional. Published in The Essence Treasury: Expressions of Gratitude. 2003.

You can contact Janet Seever at jseever1@shaw.ca

Made in the USA
Columbia, SC
30 August 2021